Bradford R. Hamann

THE GREEK DESIGN BOOK

Designs from the Age of Alexander the Great

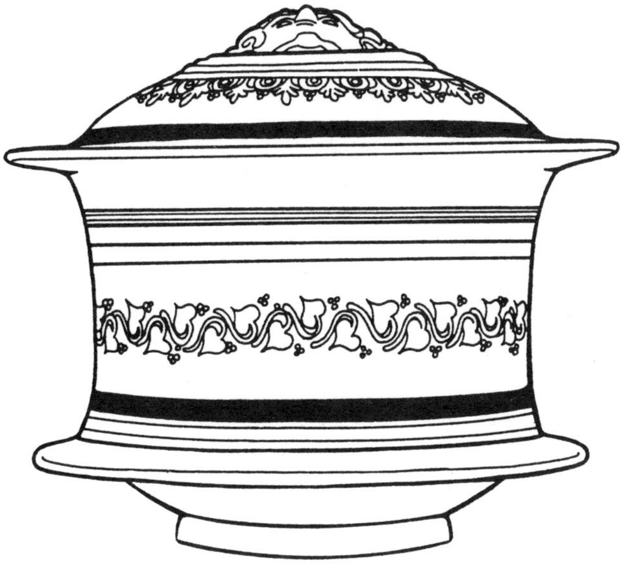

Stemmer House
PUBLISHERS, INC.
Owings Mills, Maryland

Inquiries should be directed to
Stemmer House Publishers, Inc.
2627 Caves Road
Owings Mills, Maryland 21117

Front Cover:
Krater from Derveni

Back Cover:
Gold Larnax from Vergina

A Barbara Holdridge book
Printed and bound in the United States of America

Second Printing 1983
Third printing 1990

This book is dedicated with love
to my sister, Audrey Ann Hamann,
with special thanks to
Alba Acevedo
Dayna Burnett
Alfred Wolkenberg
Ludwig Salm
Tamara Ziobert
and especially to Barbara Holdridge
for her unending patience and encouragement.

Introduction

One of the first observations of even a casual viewer of the metal work of Macedonia and classical Greece is the powerful love expressed in its decorative motifs for the things of nature. Embossed acanthus leaves of bronze swirl sensuously around the body of a sepulchre amphora. Delicate rosettes of gold, inlaid with glass the color of sea and sky, adorn the funerary container of a mighty king. Deer, lions, antelope and panthers majestically encircle the neck of a glittering krater whose handles swirl in the form of serpents. Images such as these are but part of a brilliant language of design which with fluid grace transform the functional, yielding us examples of the highest artisanship and craftsmanship.

The early Macedonians who descended from the Pindos range and settled in the region near Mount Olympus known as Pieria brought with them not only an appreciation of the flora and fauna of the land, but a fertile imagination and mystical heritage.

Thus it is that the beings and instruments of this world are intertwined with the all-powerful inhabitants of another world. We find Dionysos, Greek god of wine, life and theatre holding court as satyrs, mainads and lesser gods join in celebration. The mighty personnage of Herakles adorns a delicate perfume vase.

The pieces illustrated here are representative of a time in Greek art which saw metallurgy reach great heights. This era spanned the Classical and Hellenistic periods (5th—2nd century B.C.) and coincided with the impressive spread of political power of the Macedonian Kingdom.

Techniques of Casting and Decoration

Most of the objects presented here serve to illustrate the superior aptitude of the artistic workshops of Northern Greece for metallurgy. Two principal methods were employed in the manufacture of metalware, hammering and casting, for the latter of which Hellenistic goldsmiths knew two methods: mold casting and lost-wax casting.

Mold casting requires a mold of two or more parts of firm material which will not be damaged when the metal cast is removed.

In the lost-wax method of casting, the craftsman makes a wax prototype of the figure. He then encloses the wax figure in wet plaster-like material, into which he cuts several small channels to act as air vents. When this dries, the entire unit is heated until the wax melts and burns away. Then, melted metal is poured into the resulting mold. The cast is complete. In order to remove the finished piece, the mold must be destroyed.

The techniques employed in the decoration of metalware were quite varied. For the production of finely detailed jewelry and ornaments, the craftsman began with very thin sheets of gold. Using a rounded hammer the chunks of ingots of gold were beaten into sheets. Blanks were then cut from the sheets with chisels and worked to produce the desired shapes.

There are several methods of working sheet-gold into relief or into a figure. The first is stamping, in which one entire unit of design is punched into the metal with a hammer. Usually the metal is backed by some resilient material, such as beeswax. This method is good for shallow design work only.

The metal may also be worked freehand, from the back, into a semi-resistant material such as pitch. This technique is called repoussé, and is usually combined with chasing—essentially the same but done from the front with more delicate tools to add detail. In repoussé the gold is placed face down in warm pitch. Large areas of relief are developed by tapping the punch with a light hammer, moving smoothly and continuously over the surface to avoid an uneven or lumpy effect. When the relief has reached the desired height and shape, the piece is turned right side up in the pitch and details are chased into the simple bulged form. Much deeper relief is possible with repoussé then with stamping.

Very thin gold may also be rubbed, tapped or pressed into a die of wood, stone or clay, into which the pattern has been carved. The design may have very large or very delicate motifs.

The use of filigree or thin metal wires was prevalent. Simple round wires were made either by twisting a ribbon of gold foil, in the way that soda straws are made, or by hammering and rolling a strip of thick gold sheet until it was round. The Hellenistic goldsmiths made more complicated decorative wires by combining or twisting the simple ones in a number of different ways. They made what we call a rope by entwining two round wires; by laying side by side two ropes spiralled in opposite directions they made a "rope braid."

Granulation was another technique much used by the goldsmiths of Northern Greece. First, from a length of very fine gold wire, tiny pieces are snipped off and allowed to fall onto a block of superheated charcoal. This extreme heat causes the tiny gold bits to contract into perfect spheres. These spheres are then positioned into the design and periodically heated to fix them in place. When all granules are in place, the entire ornament is heated several times until the gold is fused into place.

Engraving involves the cutting away of a strip of metal, using a hard tool. This technique was used only for decorating large, heavy pieces, since it was not delicate enough for jewelry decoration.

Finally, the inlaying of polychromatic metals, glass and glass paste was used to enhance the beauty of the design motifs. This technique was used to color bordering petals, disks, scrolls and rosettes.

The Royal Tomb at Vergina

It was on the afternoon of November 8, 1977 that Professor Manolis Andronikos of the University of Thessalonike carefully removed a keystone from the roof of a barrel-vaulted structure he had unearthed at Vergina, a poor village in northern Greece, and looked upon the fruits of nearly forty years of hard work. What he uncovered that day would turn out to be a unique archaeological discovery.

The tomb was one of two Professor Andronikos had uncovered during excavation operations at Vergina, which he suspected had been the original site of Aegae, the capitol of Ancient Macedonia. The burial chambers were discovered while digging trenches in a large tumulus, a round structure that has been partially excavated and covered with earth. The first tomb was the smaller and had previously been looted. But apparently the grave robbers had thought this was the only tomb of the tumulus and had failed to find the other. This larger tomb was composed of a main chamber 4.46 meters square, connected to a smaller antechamber by marble doors hung from bronze bolts. It was in the large chamber that Professor Andronikos discovered a bountiful cache of assorted vessels, many of finely worked silver. These included a silver oinochoe or wine jug bearing the face of a jovial horse-eared silenus or woodland deity. Characteristic of most of the vessels found, the relief decoration is applied to the lower attachment of the handle. ***Figure 22***

Another example of this type of attachment is the head of Herakles applied to the handles of a silver alabastron or perfume vase. The face, characterized by the piercing eyes and firm-set jaw of the ancient god of strength, is framed by a lion skin which he wears as the symbol of the completion of one of his tasks. A beautiful acanthus motif is worked into the handle itself. ***Figure 19***

Also in the main chamber was a marble sarcophagus which, when opened, was found to contain a large solid gold larnax or funerary casket weighing twenty-four pounds. In it were the cremated remains of what appeared to be a Macedonian king. The lid of the casket is embossed with the sunburst emblem of the Macedonian dynasty. Its sides are profusely decorated with applied gold rosettes, some inlaid with blue glass paste, and with delicately engraved floral designs. Its legs end in powerful lion-paw feet. ***Figure 2***

Among the charred bones in the casket was found a skillfully crafted golden wreath of oak leaves and acorns. The oak was the sacred tree of Zeus; and even he, doubtless, would have been proud to wear this wreath. ***Figure 12***

Among the objects in the antechamber was a magnificent golden quiver, obviously belonging to a royal personnage. It is embossed with two bands of scenes in relief depicting the sack of a town, possibly ancient Troy. A flock of geese rises majestically above the carnage below, and the quiver is bordered with a swirling tracery of palmettes and other floral abstractions. ***Figures 27a and c***

Also in the antechamber was another golden casket, slightly smaller but with the same sunburst emblem on the lid. It was within this larnax that Professor Andronikos found a superb diadem of gold-plaited silver. The cylindrical hoop is adjustable and the surface bears an incised decoration of a "Herakles knot." ***Figure 16a***

Among the other finds which proclaimed this a tomb of importance were three gold disks embossed with the star emblem of the Macedonian dynasty, and there is a wonderfully understated elegance to be found in this trio of medallions. ***Figure 16b***

Certain clues in the form of small ivory heads and specially fitted armor gradually led Professor Andronikos to the conclusion that the tomb found at Vergina is not only a royal tomb, but that of Philip II of Macedonia, father of Alexander the Great. Regardless of whether or not future findings bear out this conclusion, the fact remains that the excavations at Vergina have unearthed a kingly treasure.

Metalwork of Thessalonike and its Surroundings

The city of Thessalonike was founded in 315 B.C. by Kassandros, king of Macedonia, and was named after the sister of Alexander the Great. Here and in the surrounding areas developed artistic workshops producing ceramic and metal objects. Because of its central location, the local craftsmen were subject to artistic influence from Ionia, Southern Greece, Athens and Corinth. Raw materials for metalworking were easily procured from the river beds and mines in the area. The impressive products of these workshops are found today in ancient graves and tombs, placed there as funerary offerings.

Perhaps the most impressive of the finds from this area is the bronze krater or wine mixing vessel featured on the front cover and found at Dervini, the site of one of numerous cemeteries in the district. The krater bears both relief decoration and applied silver ornaments. The scenes on the body of the vase depict the sacred wedding of Dionysos to Ariadne and an orgiastic ceremony of the Bacchic company. Twelve animals in relief are fastened onto the neck above a silver garland of ivy. The volute handles are richly decorated with serpents, and include palmettes, acanthus leaves and four heads of deities. On the shoulder of the krater are four statuettes representing Dionysos, a satyr and two mainads. ***Figure 1***

Also from Dervini comes a silver wine strainer with elaborate volute handles ending in goose-heads. The rim is decorated with a hatch pattern and the holes in the strainer form a graceful spiral. ***Figure 6***

An important example of jewelry includes a gold head of Herakles which was probably a pendant from an earring or other ornaments, as suggested by the flat loop at the top of the head. The workmanship which resulted in such strong modeling gives to the tiny head a monumental quality. ***Figure 7b***

A pair of gold earrings offers a stunning example of the intricate construction of Hellenistic jewelry-making. From a disk decorated in filigree with palmettes and flowers hangs a crescent-shaped ornament with elaborate floral decoration. The convex side of the crescent carries loops from which are suspended five closed flower buds and four tiny smooth fruits. The suspension system is covered by disklets decorated with flowers and inlays of glass paste. ***Figures 8 and 9***

From the quarters of present-day Stavroupolis which contain the cemeteries of ancient Thessalonike comes a gold ornament whose heraldic composition comprises acanthus leaves and spiral tendrils with palmette finials on either side. ***Figure 25a***

Found at Neapolis — another cemetery site — among other ancient treasures, was a pair of bracelets of twisted gold wire ending in antelopes' heads. One of these is illustrated here. ***Figure 17***

These objects serve to illustrate the artistic achievements of the metalsmiths working in this area in the Age of Alexander.

Amphipolis (Eastern Macedonia)

Amphipolis was founded by the Athenians in 438 B.C. and became part of the Macedonian Kingdom in 359 B.C. Philip II took special care to install a strong Macedonian element in the city, and it was from its harbor that Alexander's fleet sailed for the expedition to Asia. Excavations in the area of Amphipolis, begun in 1956, have uncovered a necropolis as well as other large sections of the city's structure. The splendid gold jewelry found in this necropolis suggest the existence of local workshops of miniature art in Amphipolis. Pieces recovered include the gold diadem of a plain long strip set with a central "Herakles knot." The knot is decorated with rosettes, which show traces of a blue glass paste. ***Figure 10a***

Also found was a gold finger-ring with hoop composed of strips and rhomboidal bezel, inset with a dark-brown garnet. Two serpents, winding around the hoop, meet at the two corners of the bezel, with heads and tails in heraldic arrangement. ***Figure 18***

Unearthed at Amphipolis was a pair of gold earrings of Ionian type, in pyramidal form. The lavish filigree decoration is comprised of palmettes, spirals and beads. The edges and corners are ornamental with applied gold pellets. ***Figure 20***

Abdera (Thrace)

Abdera was an Ionian colony founded in 545 B.C. near the mouth of the river Nestos, by settlers from Teos in Asia Minor. The city flourished mainly in the Archaic and Classical periods. Excavations began in 1950, and among the items recovered was a beautiful string of gold beads, some plain and some decorated with filigree. ***Figure 10b***

Beroia (Western Macedonia)

One of the cities that grew in the fertile Macedonian plain was Beroia, where life has continued without interruption from the Classical period to the present time.

From Beroia comes an exquisite pair of gold earrings. Each hook is covered with plaited chain and terminates in the figure of Aphrodite worked in the round. The goddess is depicted nude, her ears, arms, ankles, and breasts adorned with jewelry. The goddess of love and beauty, Aphrodite was the daughter of Zeus. With the help of a magic girdle she was able to arouse love in others. Here she displays her charms with complete confidence, showing us why others could so easily fall under her spell. ***Figure 7a***

Additional Designs From the Age of Alexander

Other objects illustrating the skill of Macedonian craftsmen include the following:

Matrix and cast of clay figurine representing Cybele from Olynthus.

Mother of Hades, Poseidon and Zeus, Cybele was one of the most revered and powerful Greek gods. Stately and dignified, she wears a crown whose shape brings to mind a series of towers and battlements, an allusion to her majestic status. Both crown and earrings are decorated with stylized acanthus leaves, and she wears a necklace of acorns. ***Figure 11***

Clay box of the Hellenistic period (pyxis).

The lid is decorated with concentric circles enclosing the relief head of Medusa. A circle of palmettes and smaller circles surround the head. The side of the box is decorated with several solid bands and a band of abstract heart-shaped leaves. ***Figures 13 and 21***

Marble column capital of the Ionic order. ***Figure 3***

Leg of marble bed from the Macedonian tomb of Kerdyllion. ***Figures 4 and 5***

Bronze knocker in the form of a lion-head holding in its mouth a ring with grooves. From Olynthos. ***Figure 23***

Gold circlet, probably part of the decoration on the hilt of a sword. It is ornamented with eight palmettes (two are missing), spreading radially from a central multi-petaled rosette. From Stavroupolis, Thessalonike. ***Figures 24a and c***

Gold necklace composed of a chain and a central small plaque of oval shape with filigree decoration and inset dark red garnet. Neapolis, Thessalonike. ***Figure 24b***

Two gold earrings of twisted wire ending in a cylindrical setting, decorated with lanceolate leaves. The setting supports a miniature Negro head made out of hard red-black stone. The skull is covered by gold foil with embossed rendering of the Negro's hair. Hagios Athanasios, Thessalonike. ***Figure 25b***

Design band derived from two necklaces of gold discovered at Derveni. ***Figure 26***

Gold fibula with its catch-piece. Derveni. ***Figure 27b***

Portrait of Alexander (reconstructed by the artist for the purposes of this book), from a mosaic — a Roman copy of a Greek painting — depicting his victory over the Persians. ***Figure 28***

Handle attachment to a silver hydria in the shape of a siren. The eyes are inlaid with silver, and the handle terminates in a cut-out floral composition of acanthus and spirals. ***Figure 29***

Pair of gold earrings from Palaiokastron. The upper and lower disks are inlaid with garnets; the lower disks are flanked by rounded extensions, each supporting a wired pearl in a bezel setting. The central pendants are in the form of two erotes. ***Figure 30***

Spiral bracelet of gold in the form of two snakes, their heads pointing in opposite directions, and their tails tied together in a Herakles knot, in the center of which is a large oval garnet in a bezel setting, around the base of which there is laid a beaded wire. From Eretria. ***Figure 31***

Gold necklace whose two terminals are in the shape of snake heads. A large acorn pendant is suspended from a triple rosette. ***Figure 32***

Gold ornament probably worn on the breast. It consists of four gold bands joined together by an oval bezel inset with a dark brown garnet. From Abdera. ***Figure 33***

Gold ornament for the thigh, with a Herakles knot and two female heads in the round. Abdera. ***Figure 34a***

Gold finger ring. The hoop is attached to the bezel with minute lion heads. The bezel, in the shape of a Boiotian shield, is decorated with a central Gorgoneion flanked by palmettes. Eleutheres, Kavala. ***Figure 34b***

Gold diadem of oak leaves mounted on two oblong strips, which are attached to a central disk embossed with a Medusa head. ***Figure 34c***

Handle and spout design of a bronze situla from Kozani. ***Figure 35a***

Handle and mouth design of a bronze oinochoe from Kozani. ***Figure 35b***

Gold earrings with cupids suspended from disks ornamented with filigree rosettes. From Abdera. ***Figures 36 and 37***

Handle design from bronze krater. The volute handles are ornamented with smaller volutes and palmettes, and are attached to the shoulder of the vase with goose heads. The rim is decorated with an Ionic cymatium. From Derveni. ***Figure 38a***

Silver plaques embossed with lion heads. ***Figure 38b***

Bronze amphora lid, with a movable arched handle for suspension, held by rings attached to the tops of the two main handles. From Derveni. ***Figure 39a***

Silver plaques embossed with lions' heads. ***Figure 39b***

Ornaments from a gold necklace found at Pelinnaion, Trikala. They include two crescents, a rosette and two medallions with the busts of Helios (Sun) and Selene (Moon). ***Figure 40***

Pair of dolphin-shaped earrings with rosette eyes. ***Figure 41***

Medallion-disk: Bust of Athena. The emblem is framed by a wreath assembled from seven garnet segments. ***Figure 42***

Medallion disk: Bust of Eros. The bust shows the child-god fullface. He is characterized as a winged Bacchanalian with ivy and grape leaves, as well as two clusters of ivy berries in his hair. ***Figure 43***

Attachment in the shape of the goat god Pan, from a bronze lantern found at Vergina. ***Figure 44***

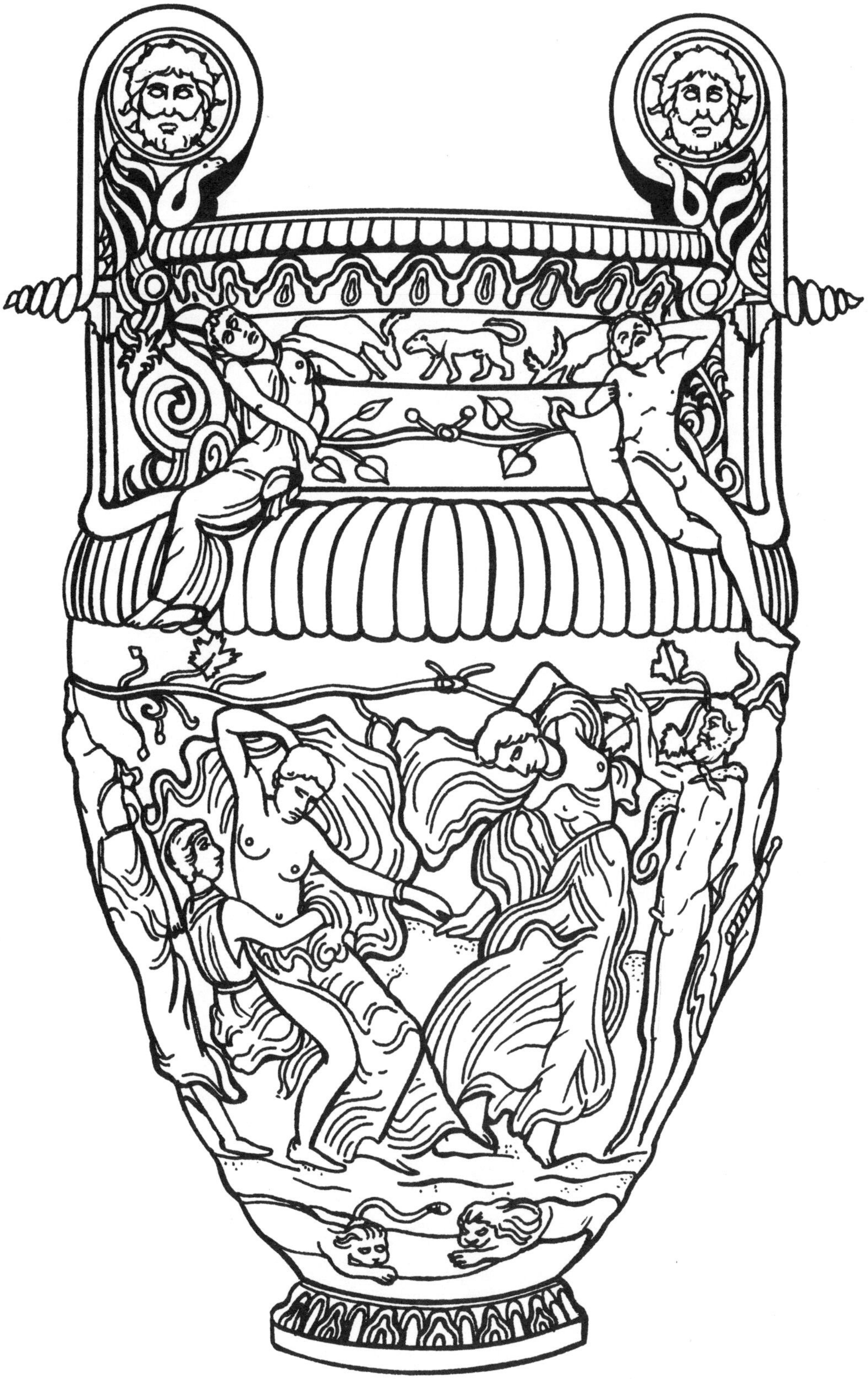

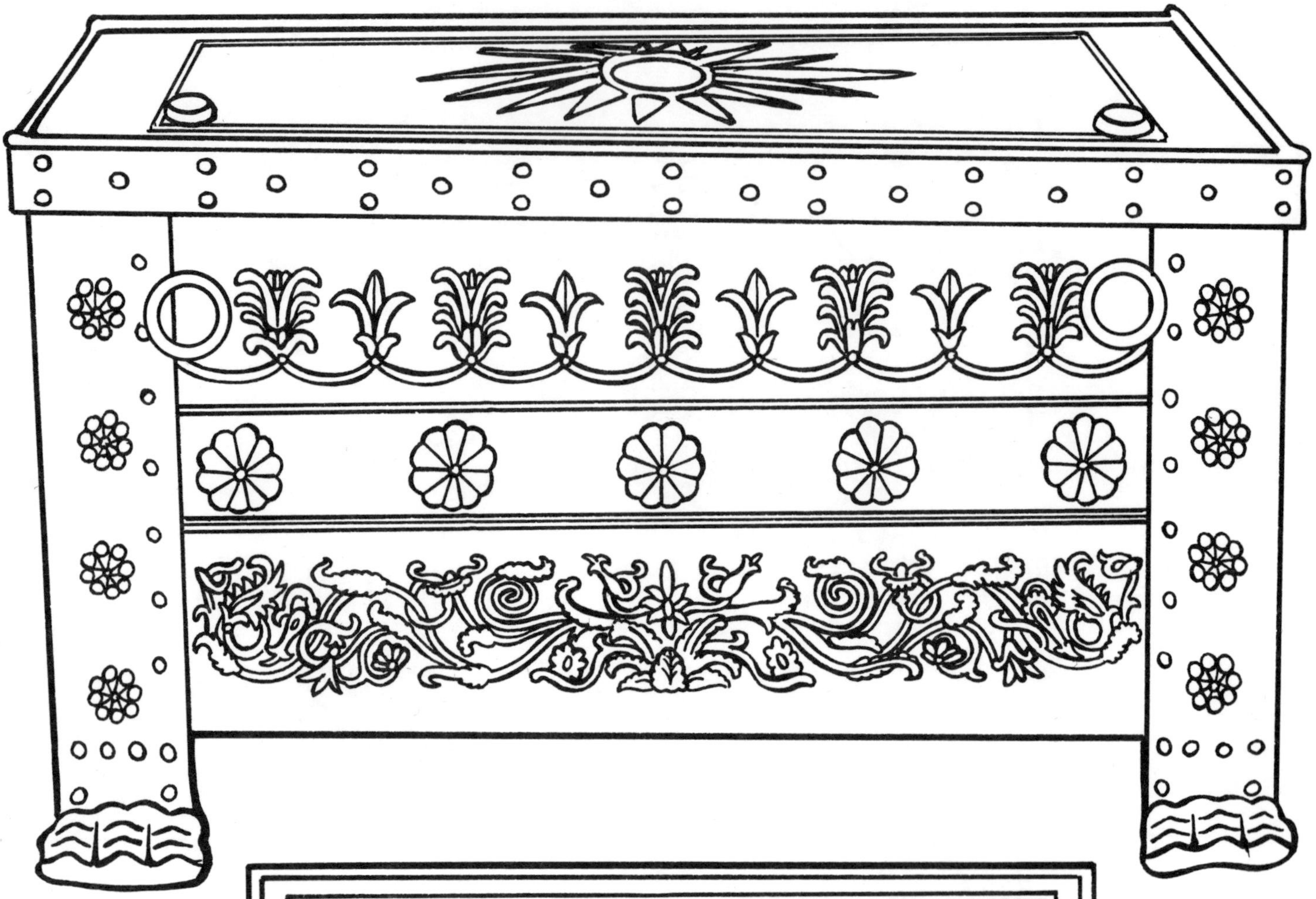

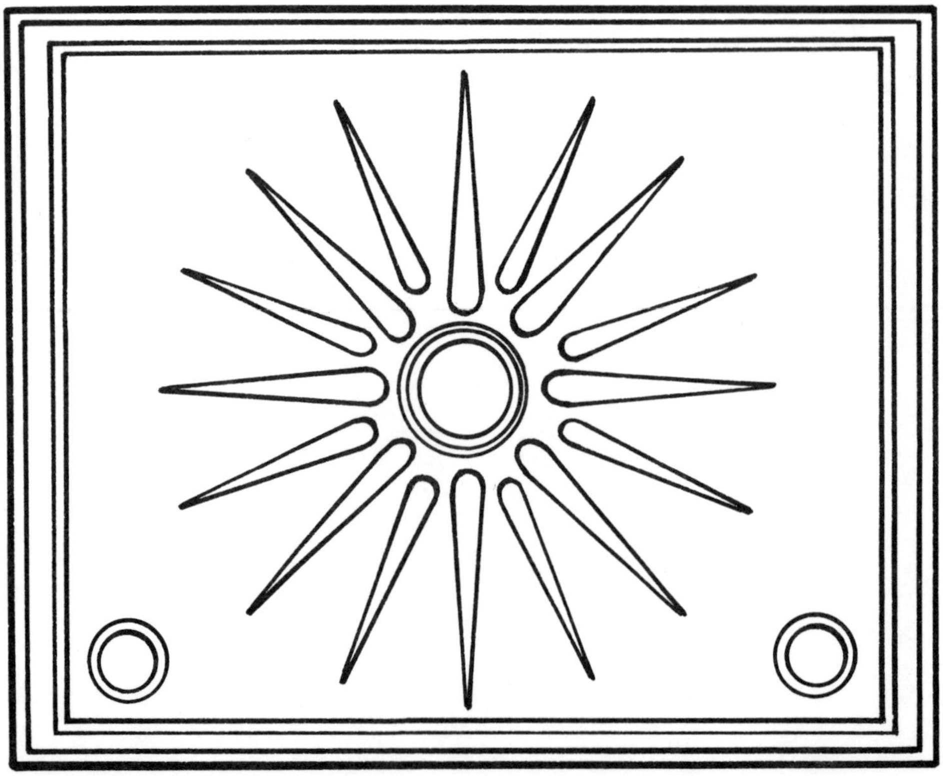

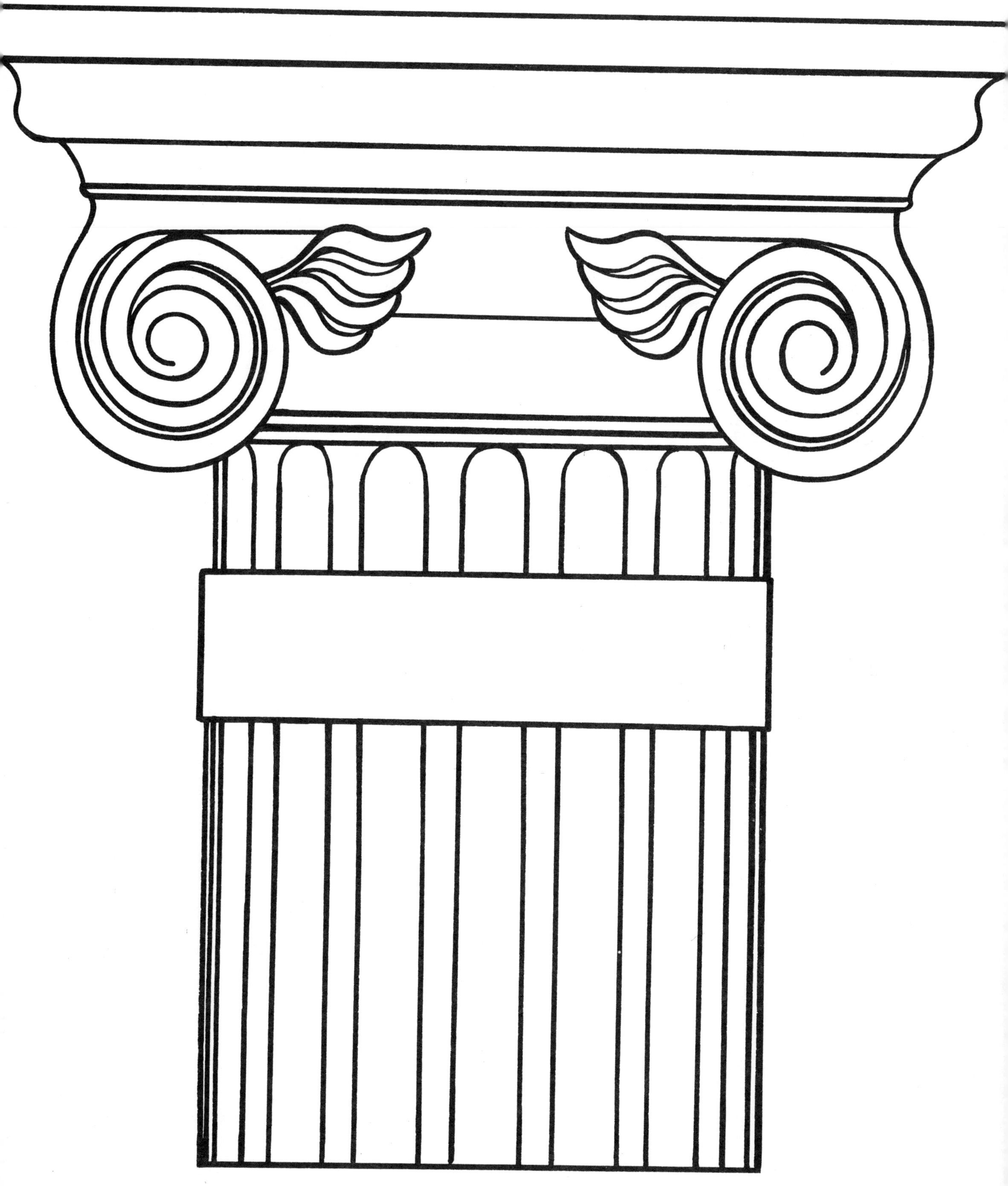

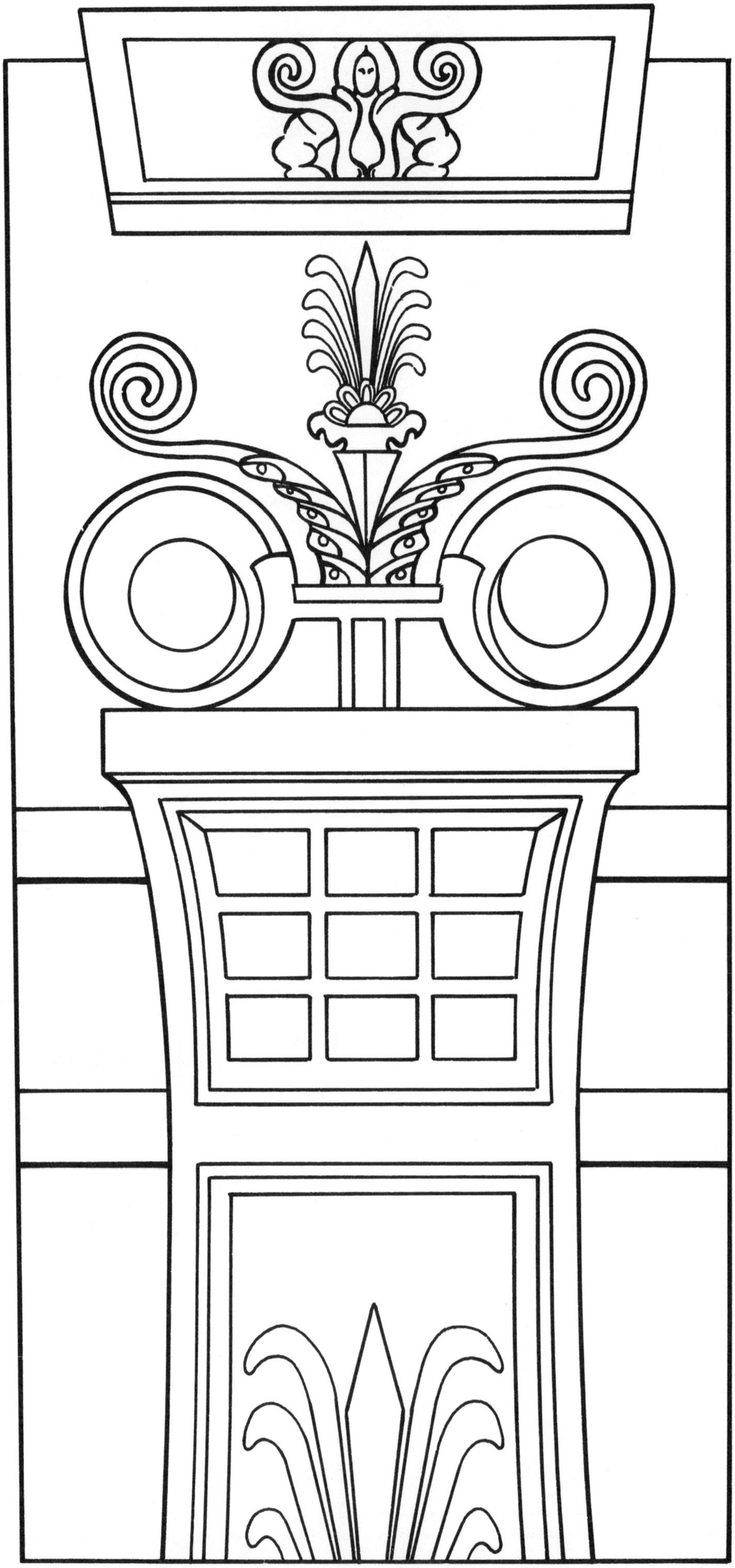

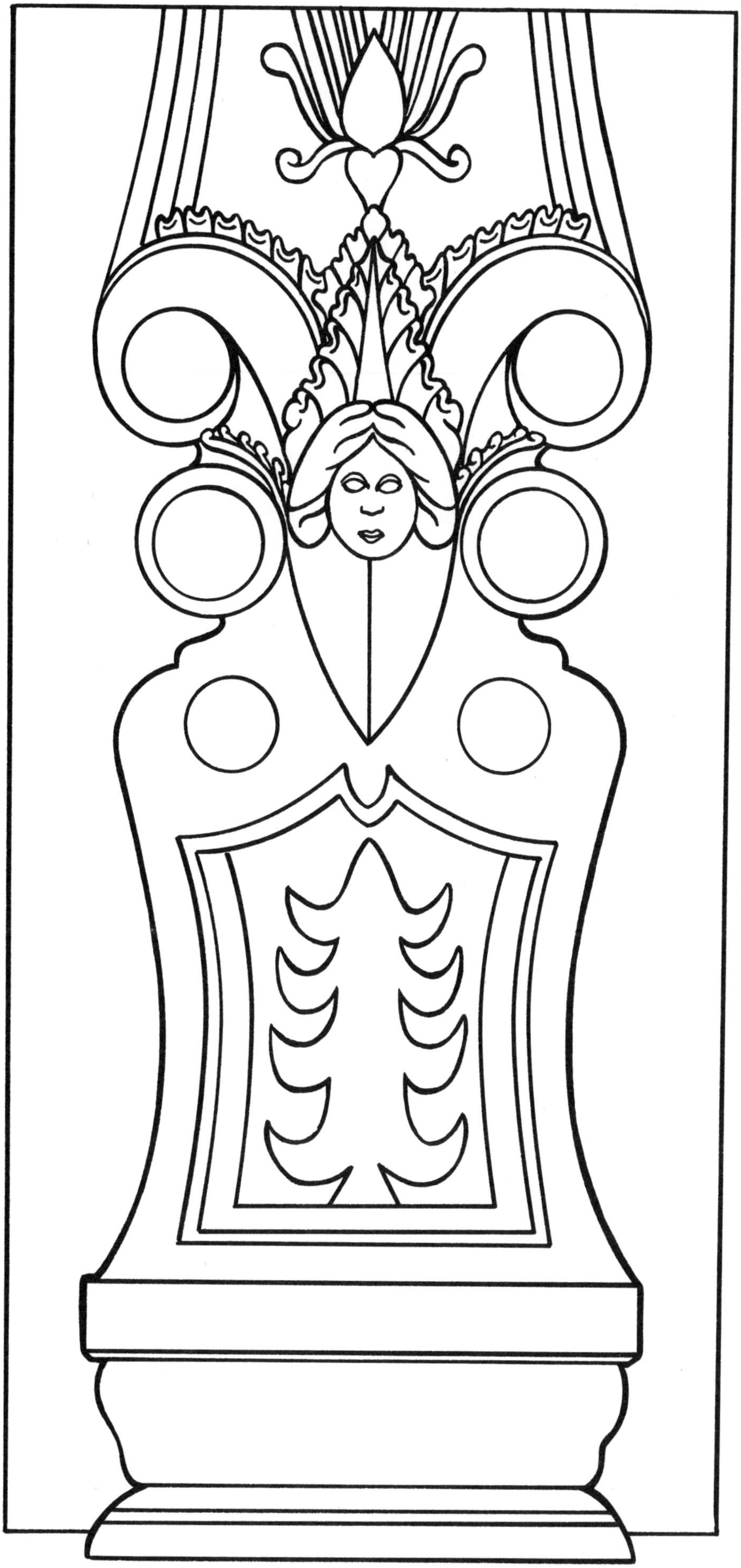

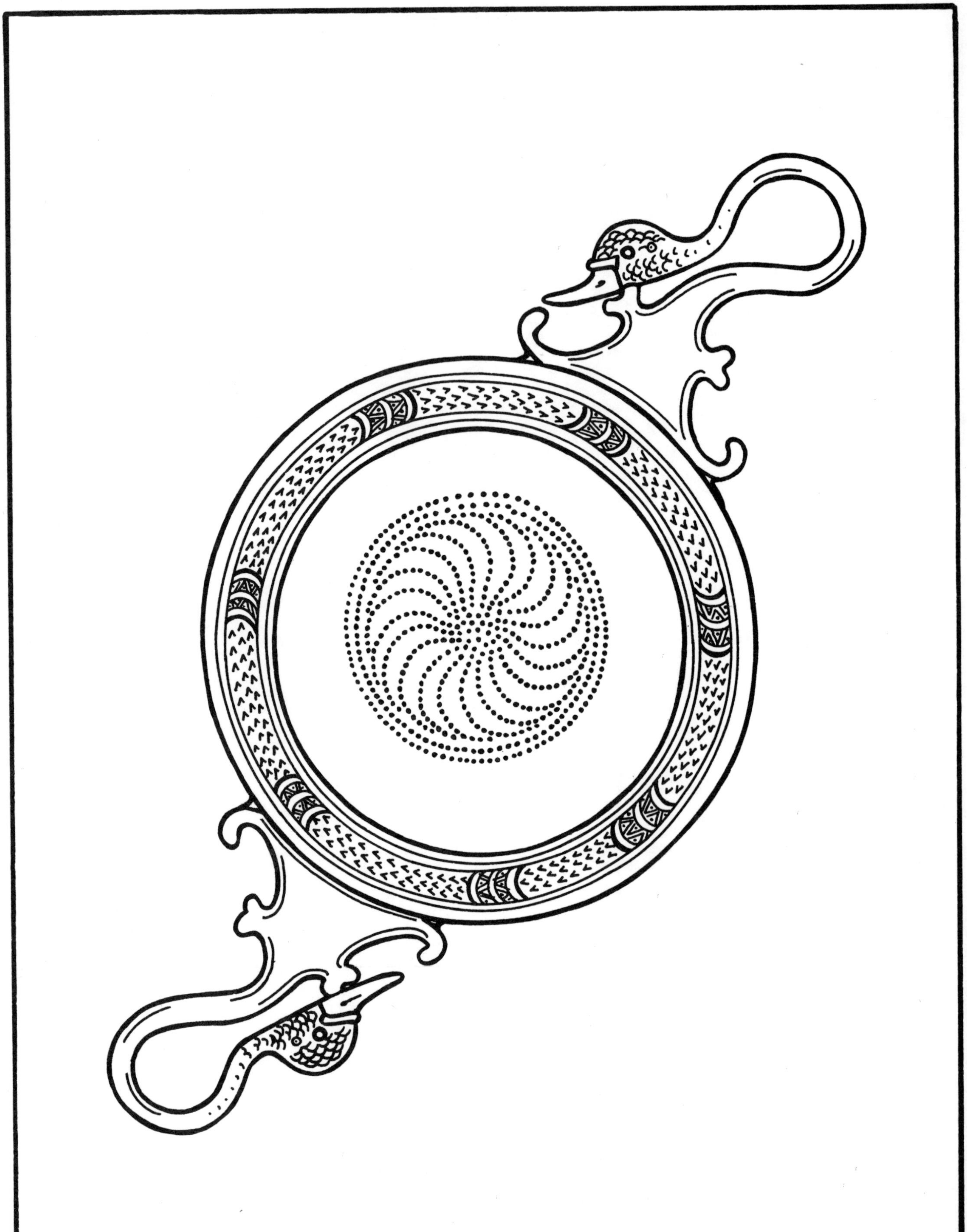

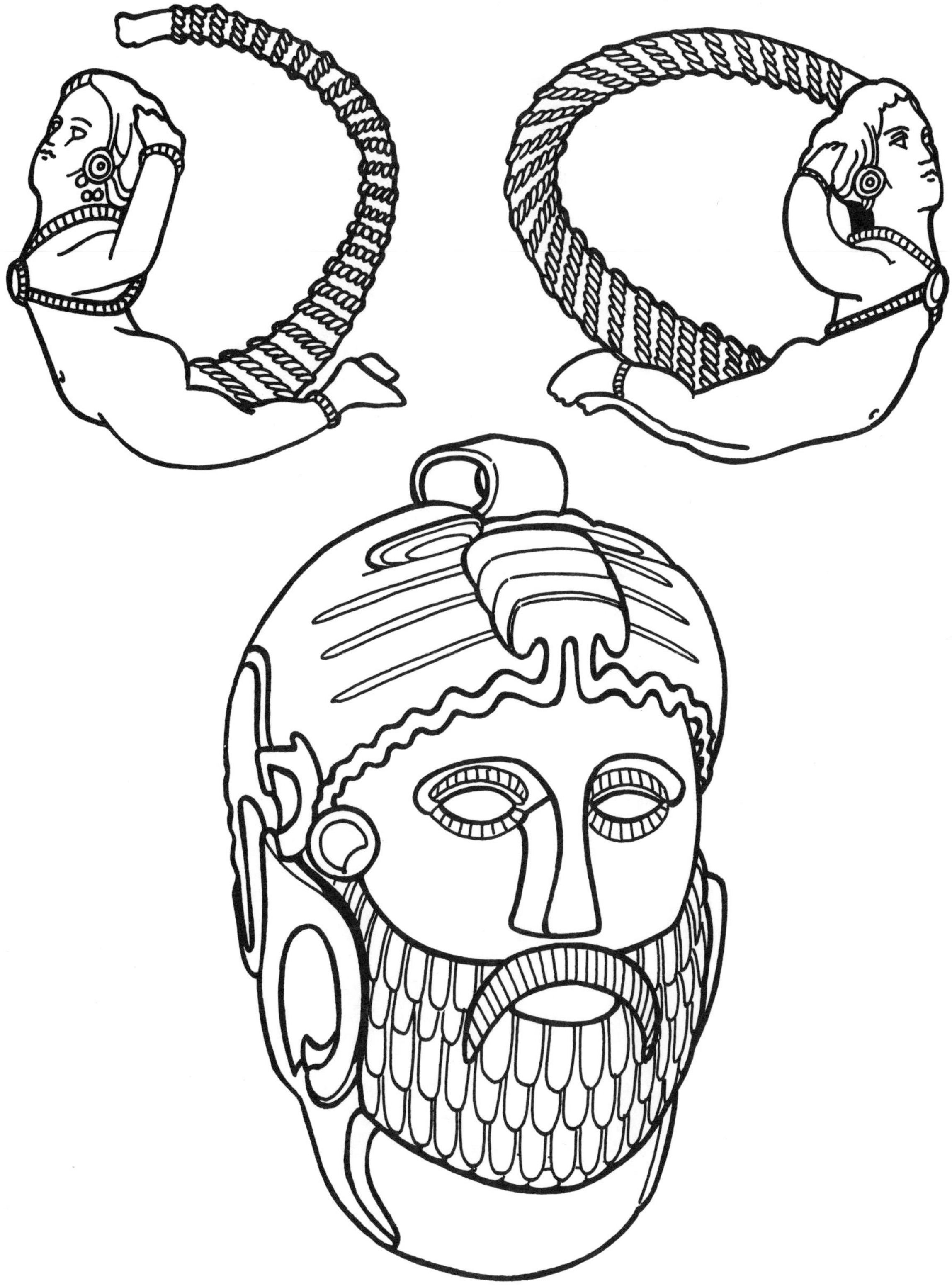

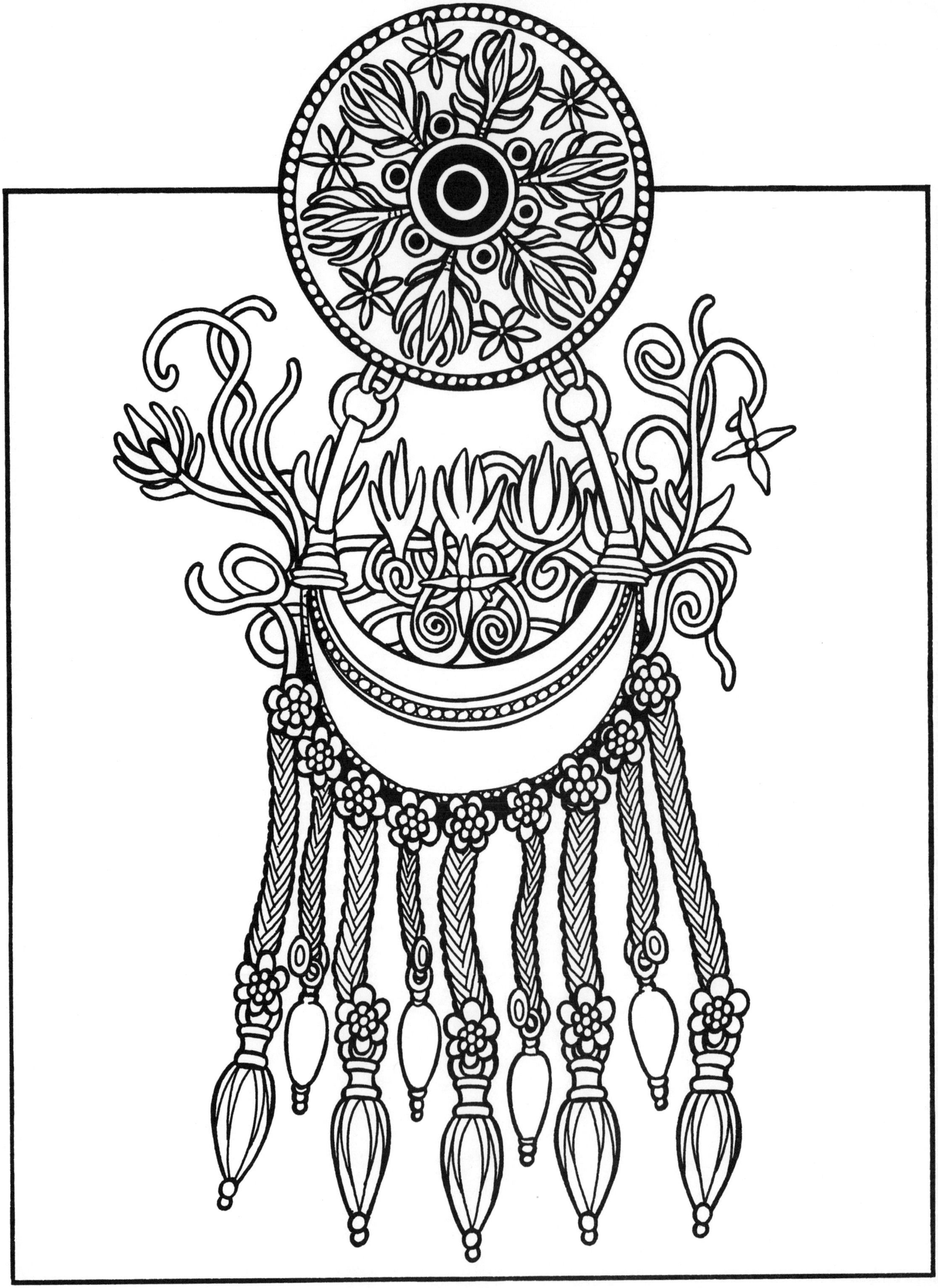

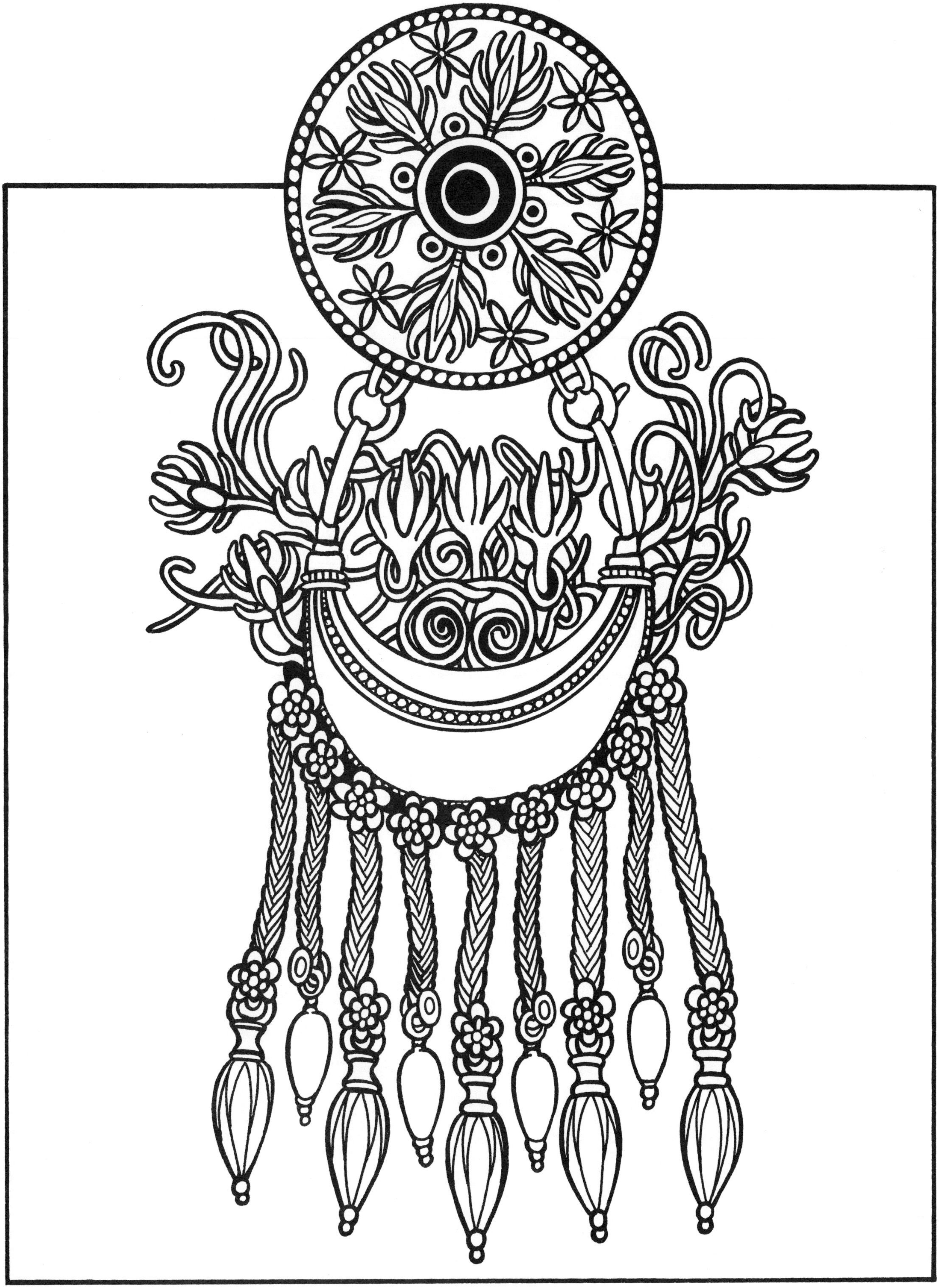

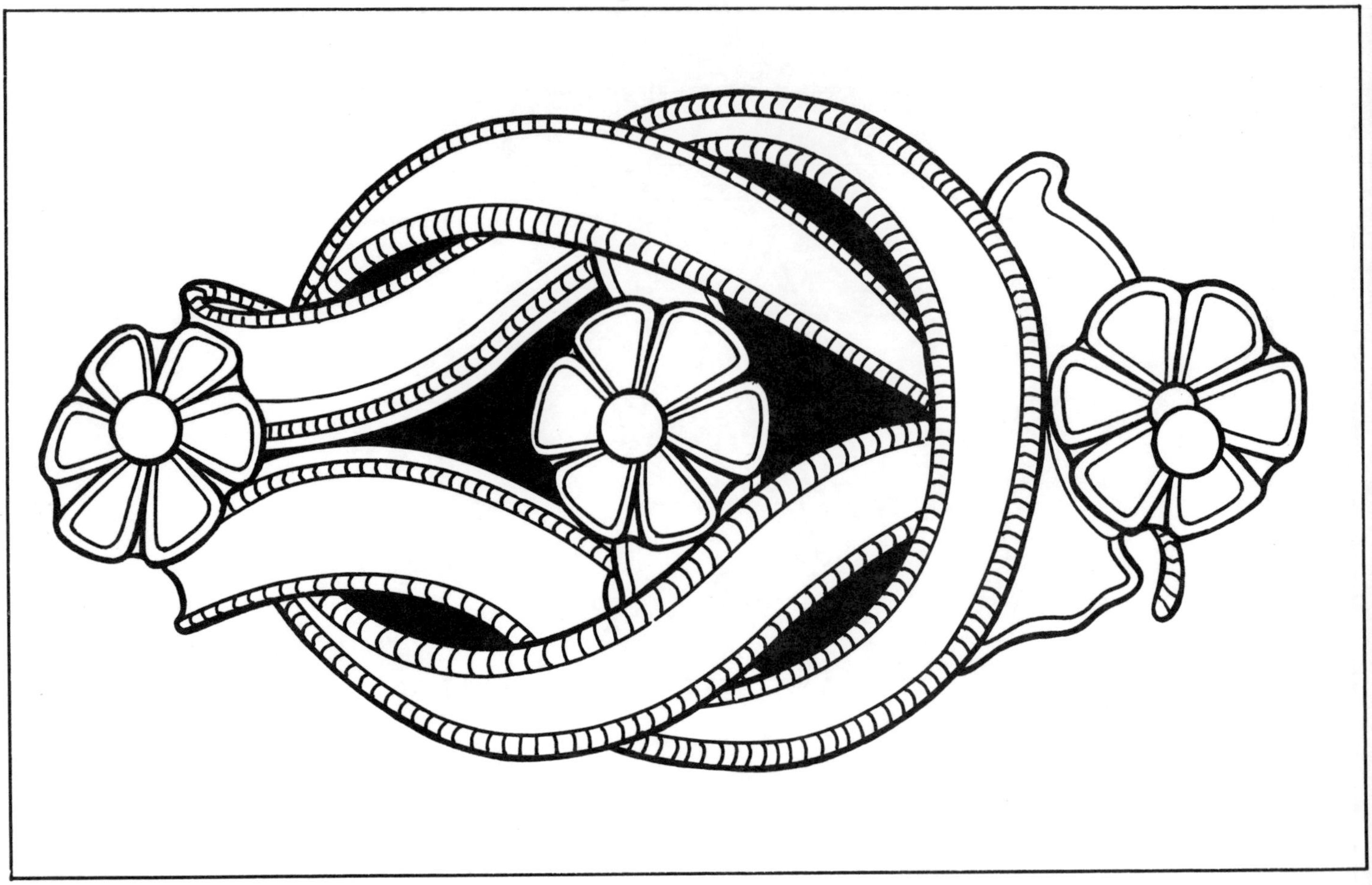

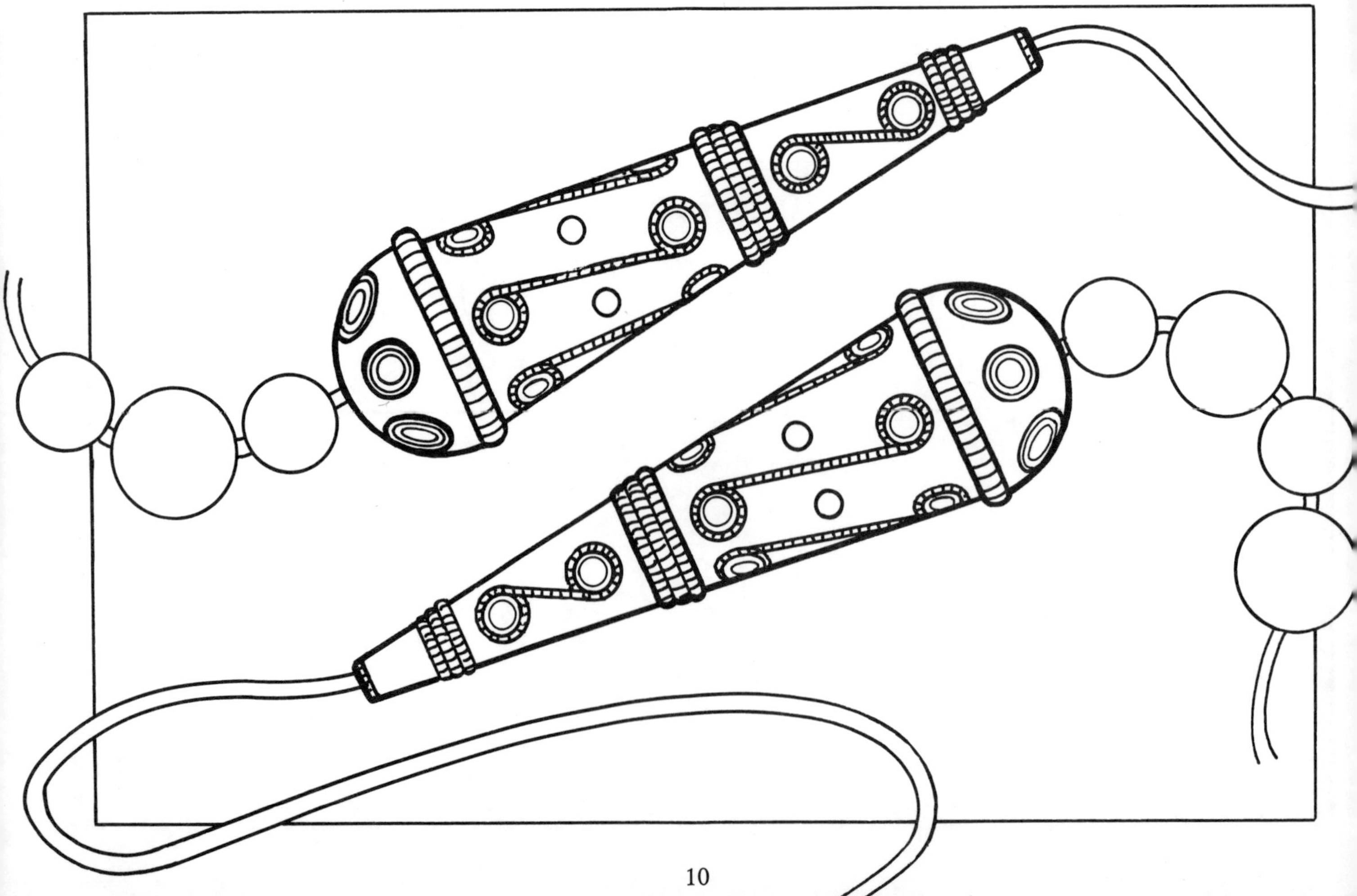

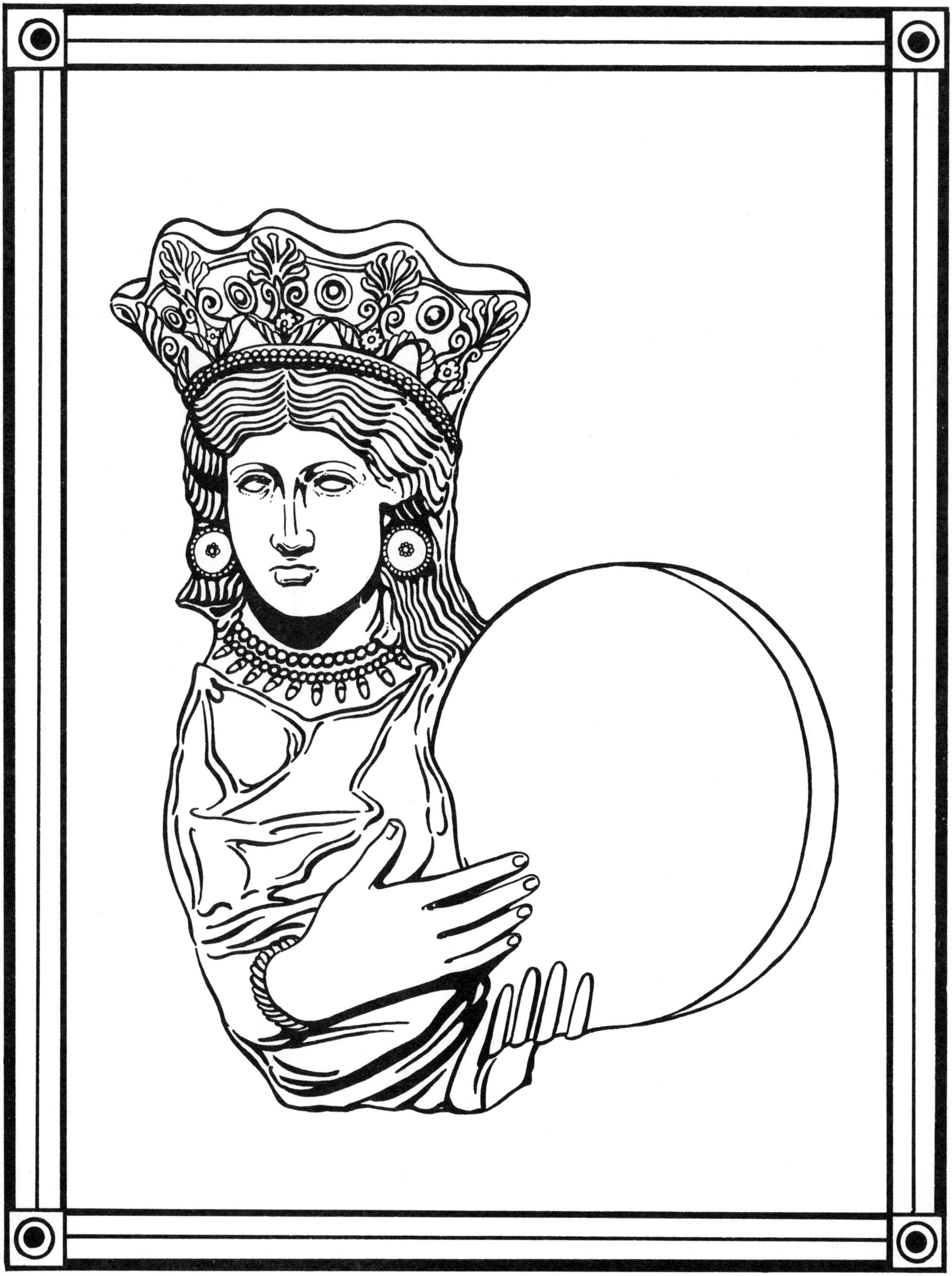

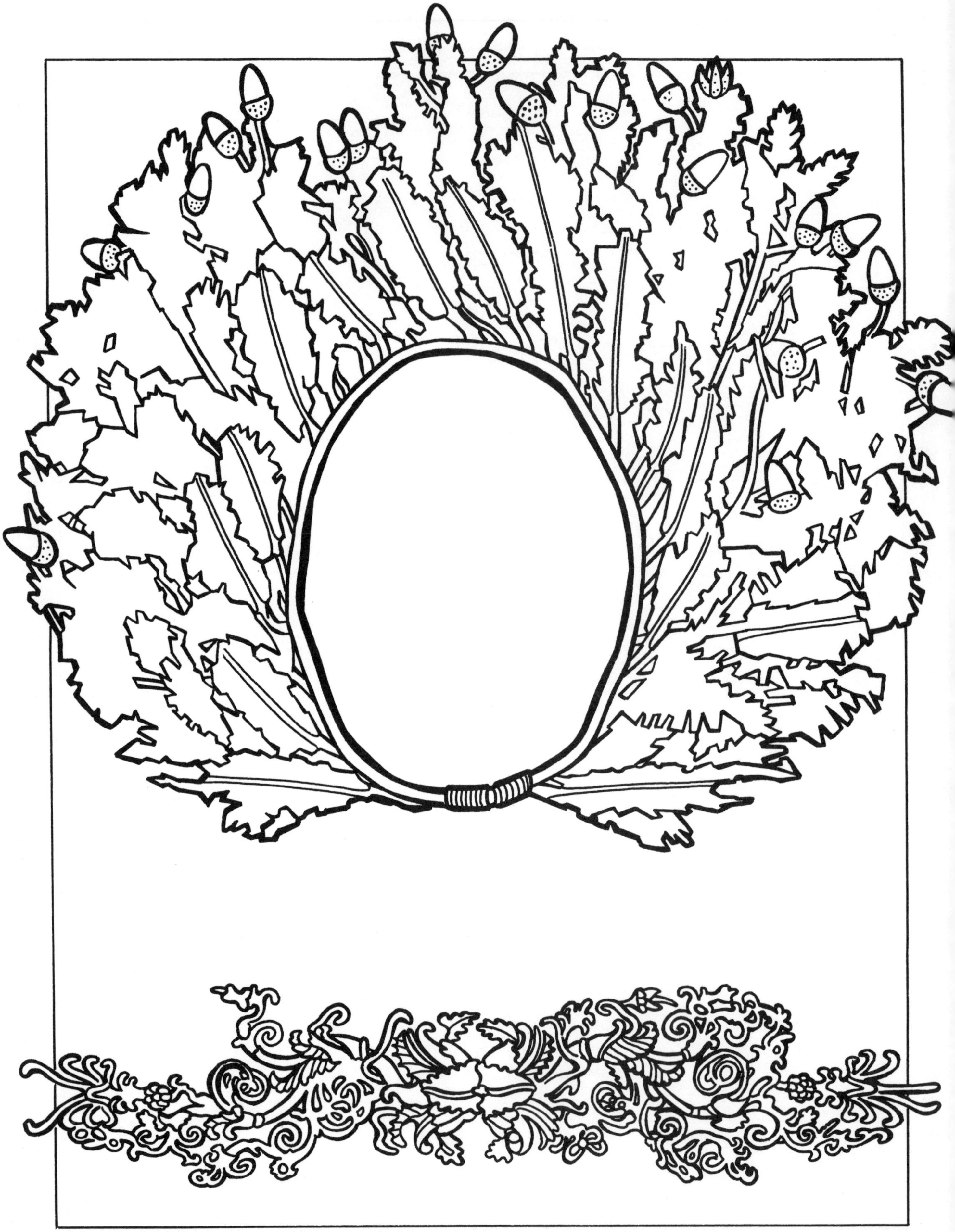

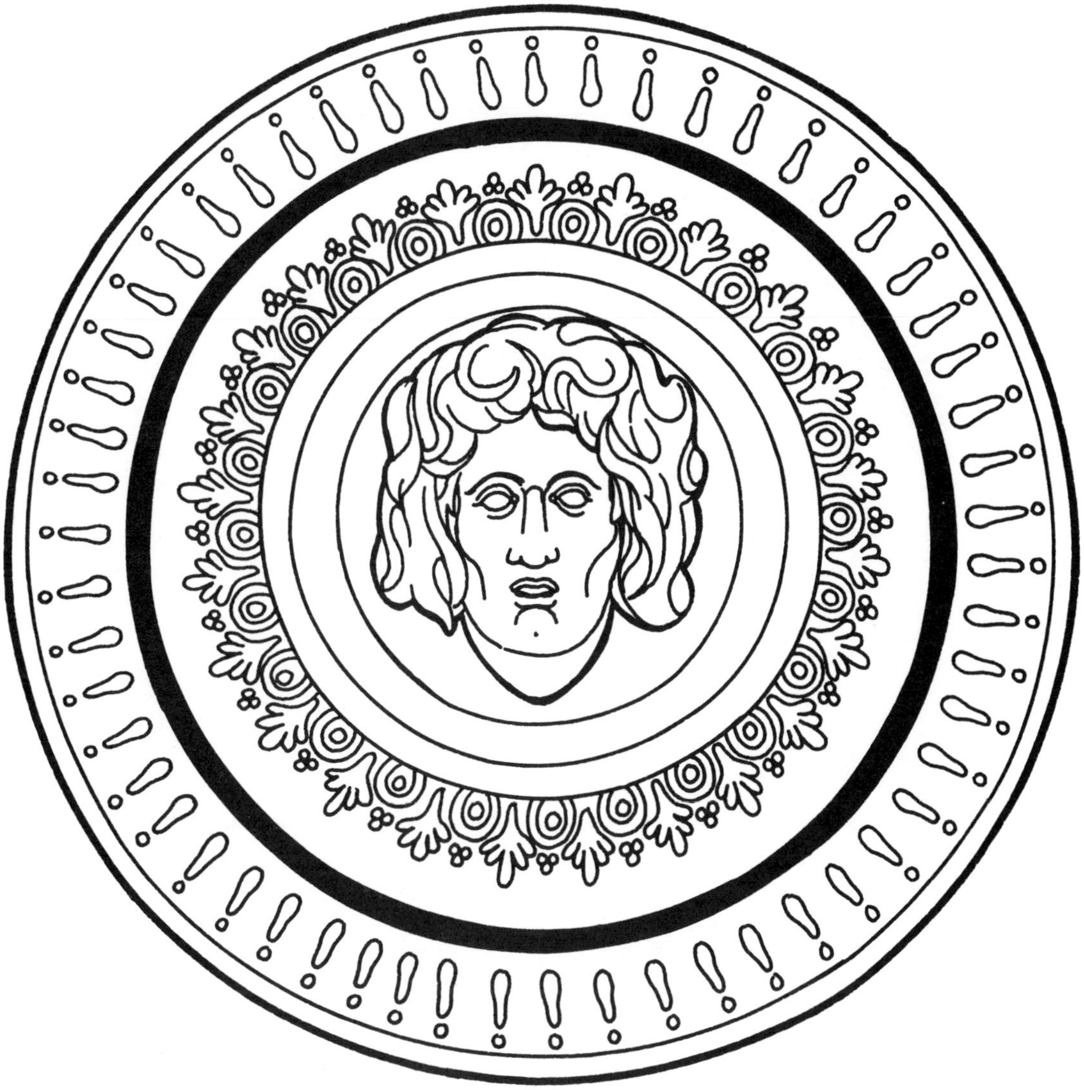

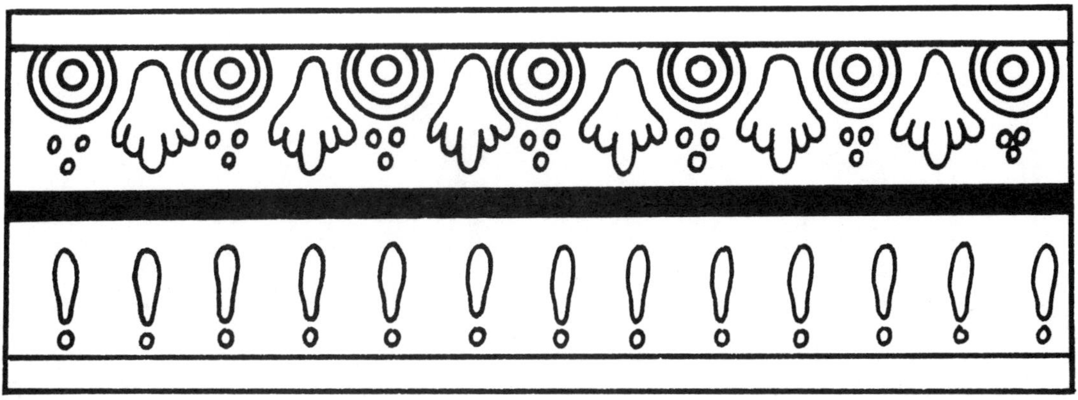

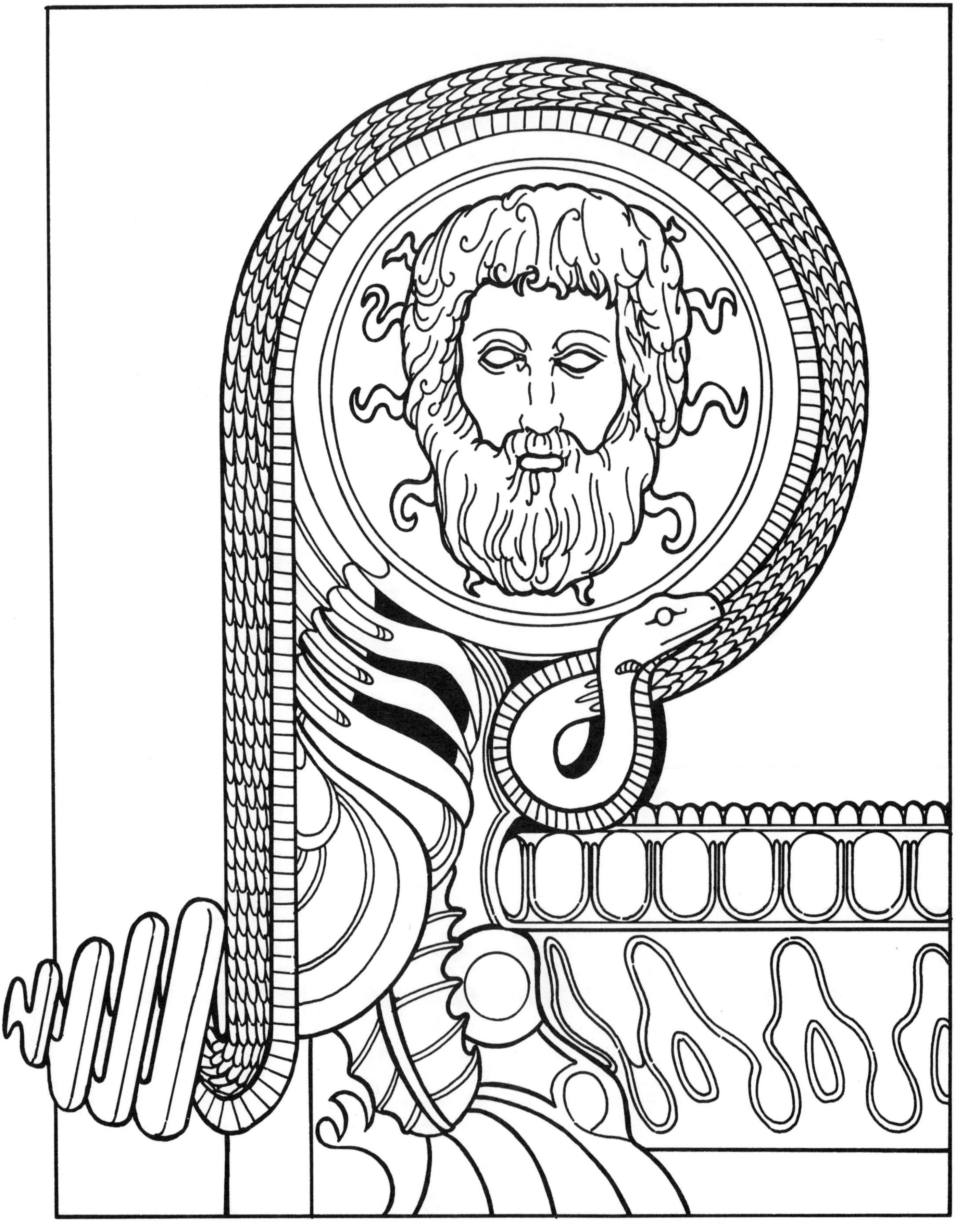

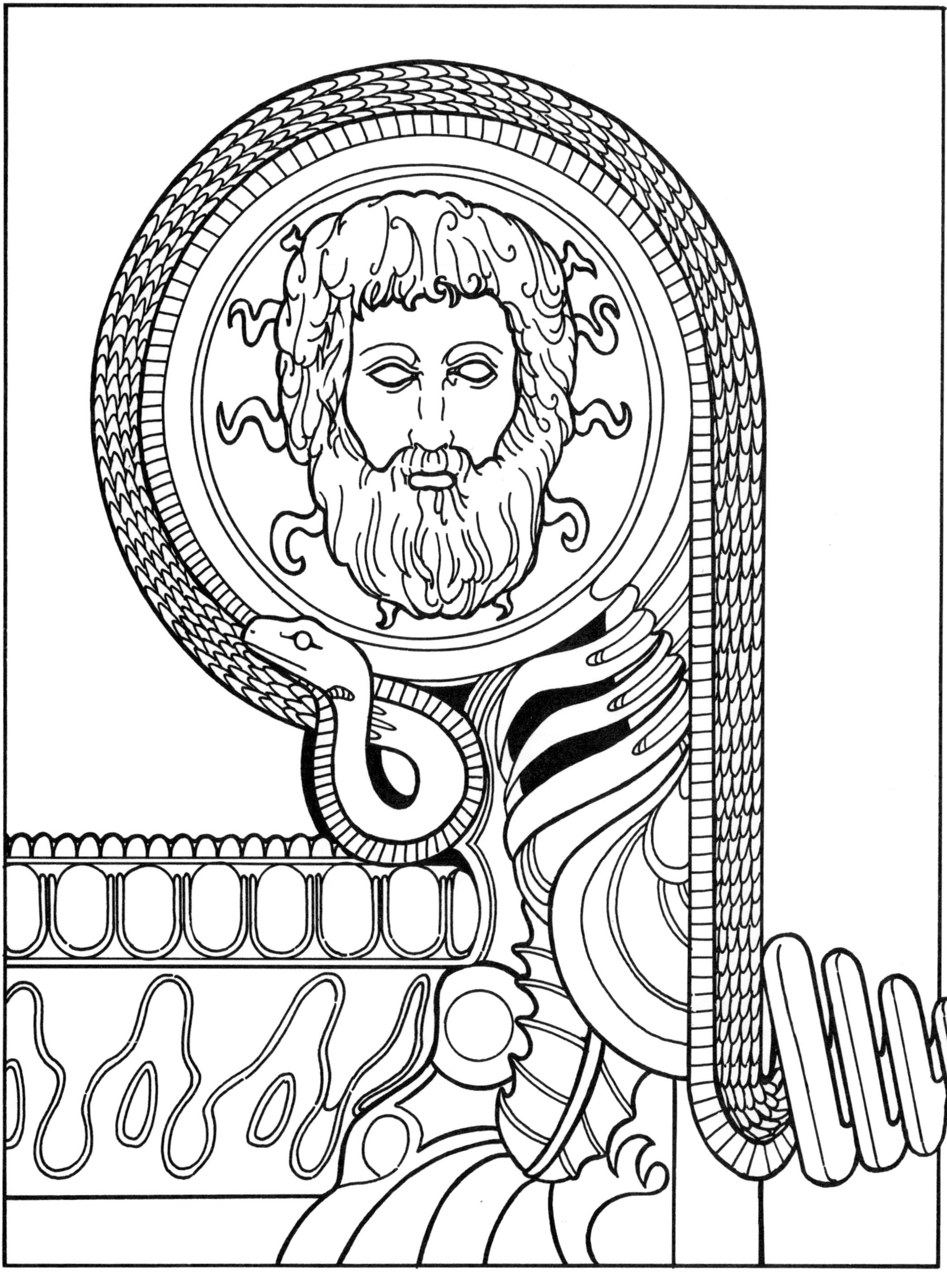

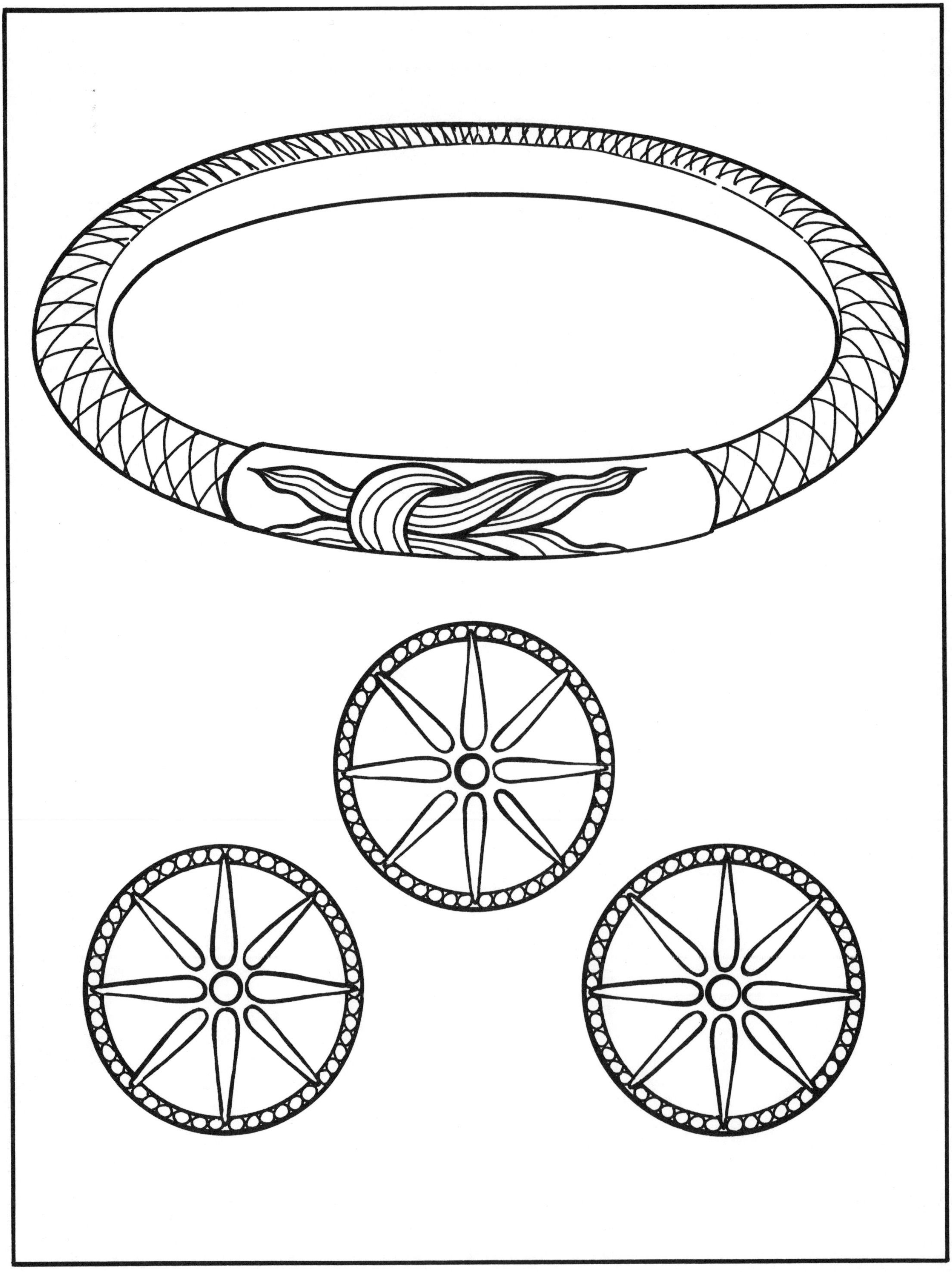

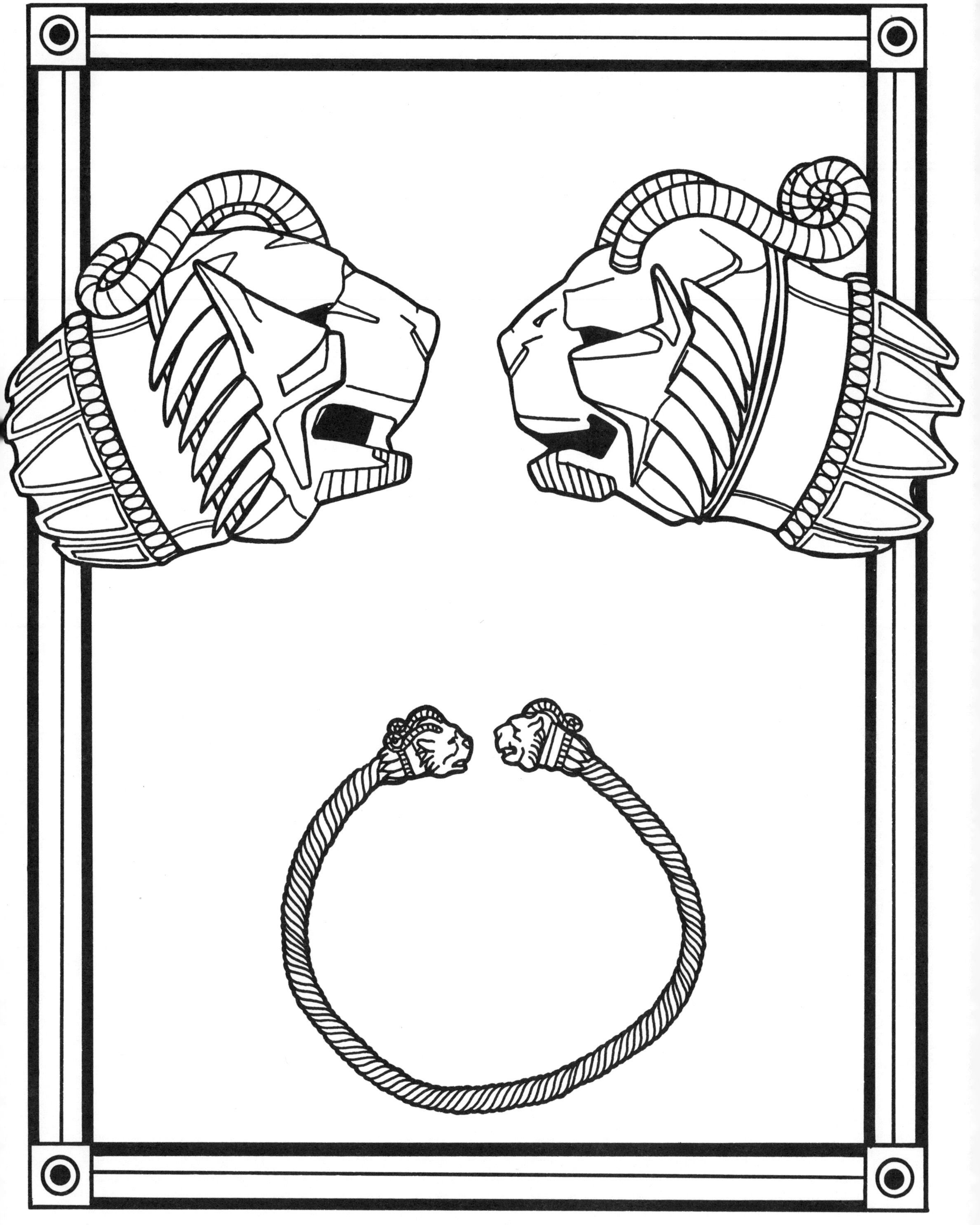

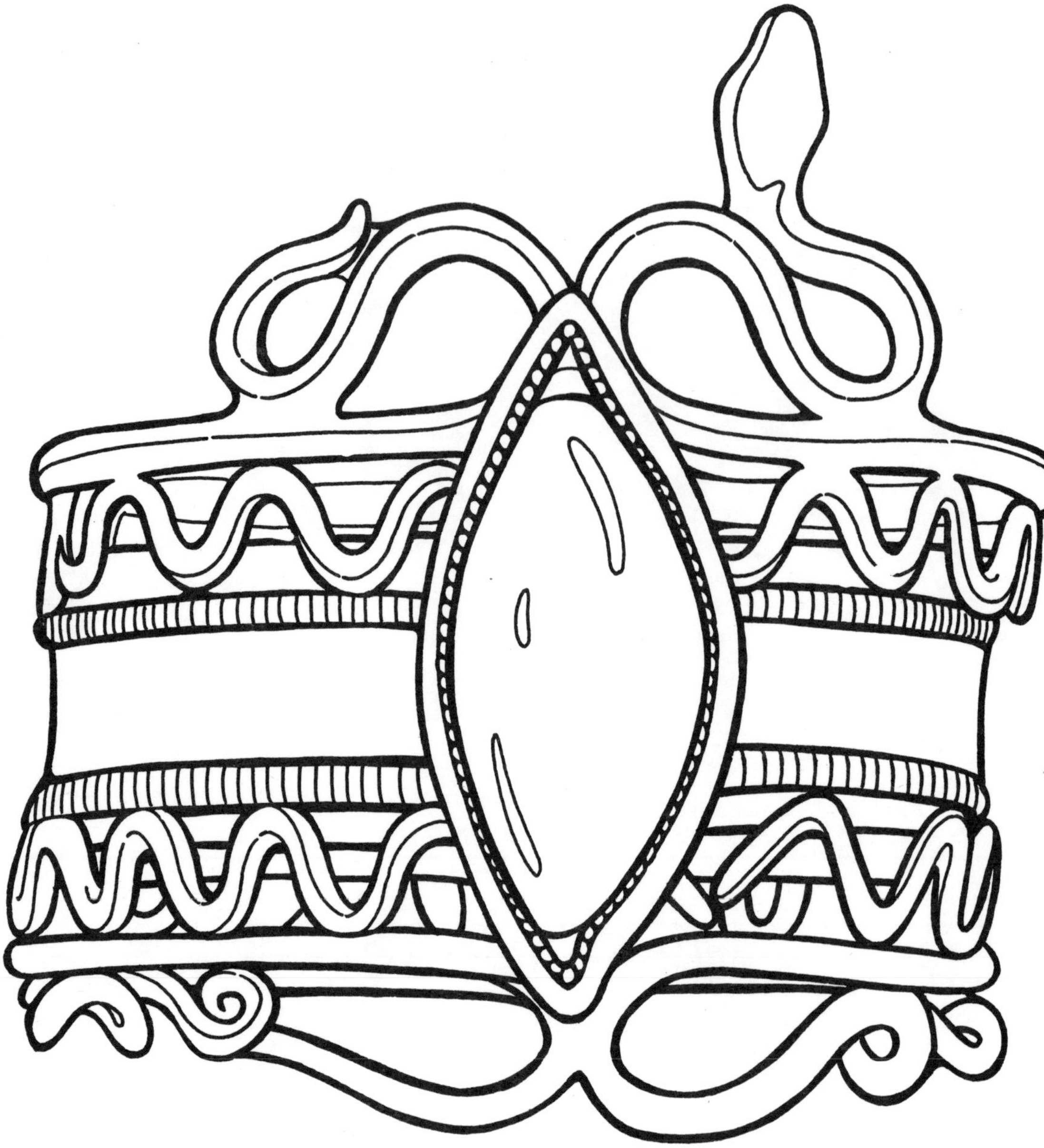

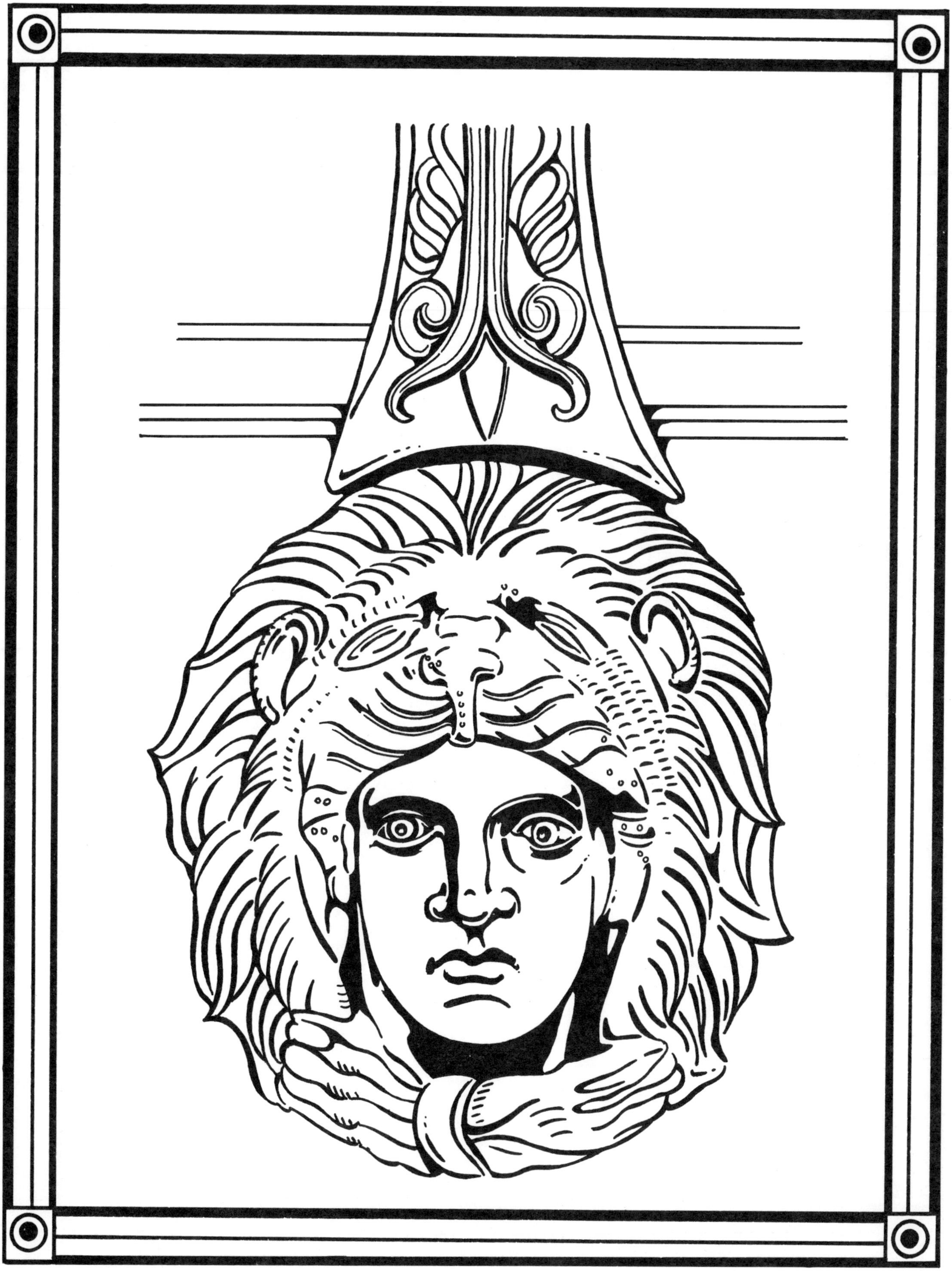

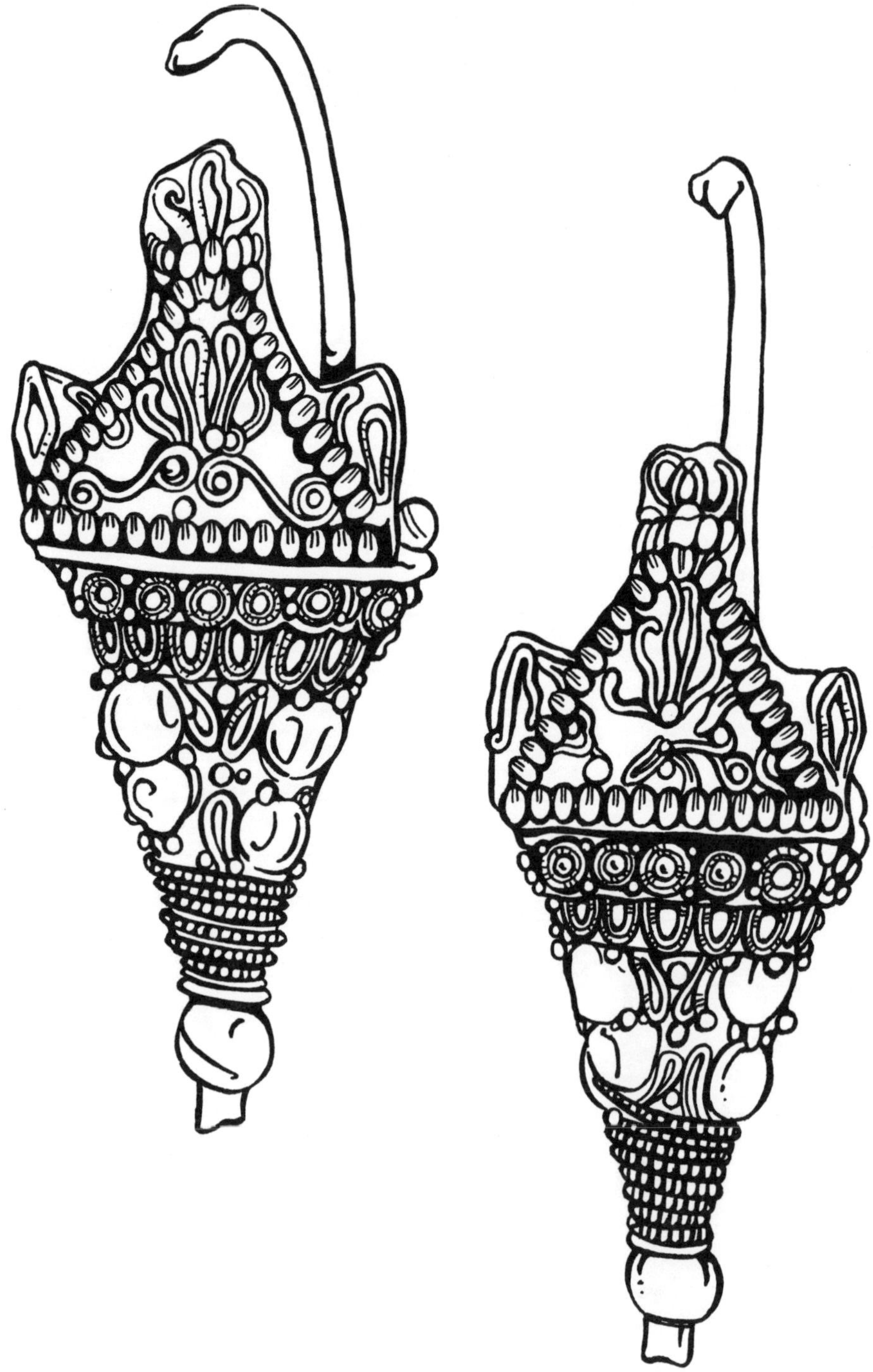

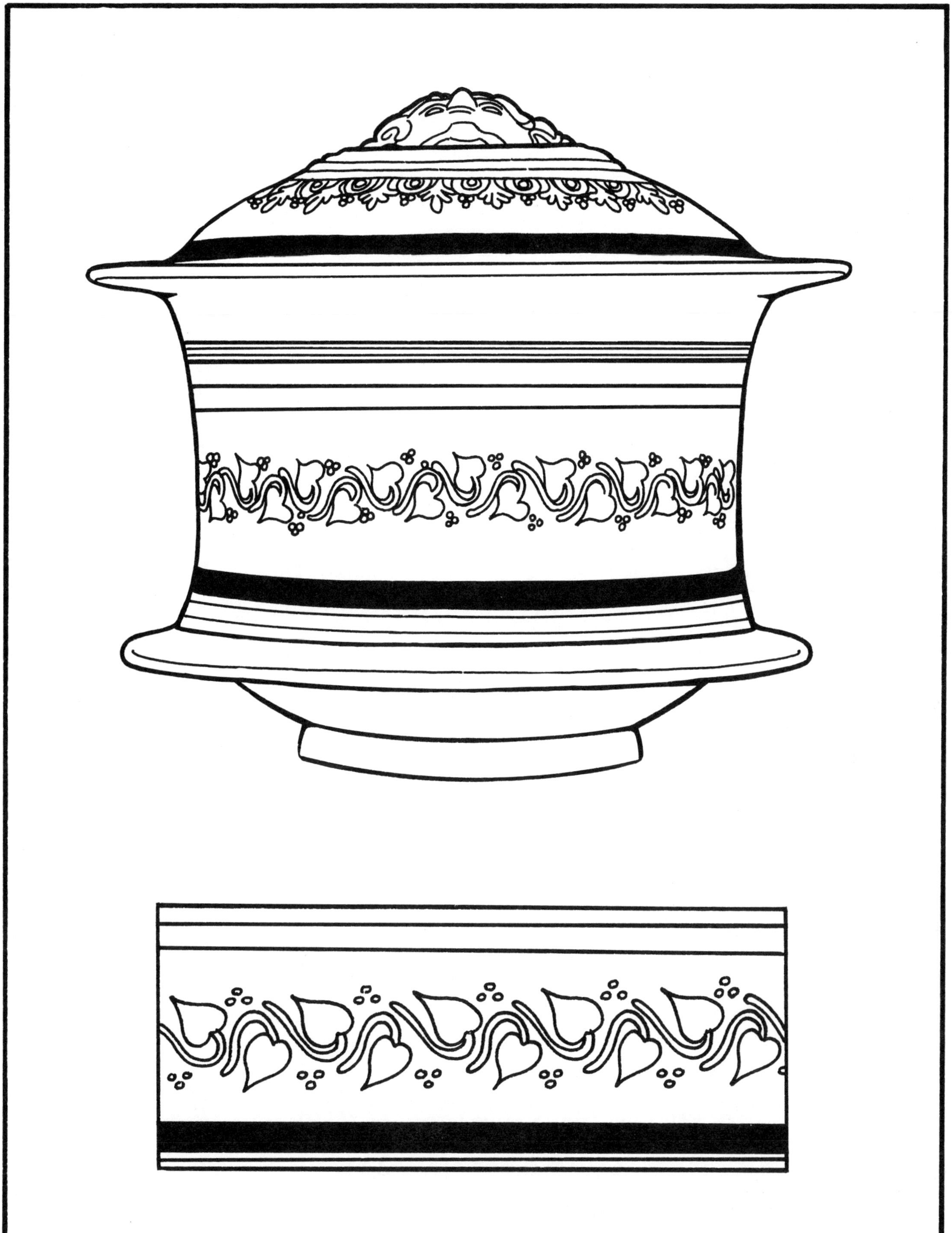

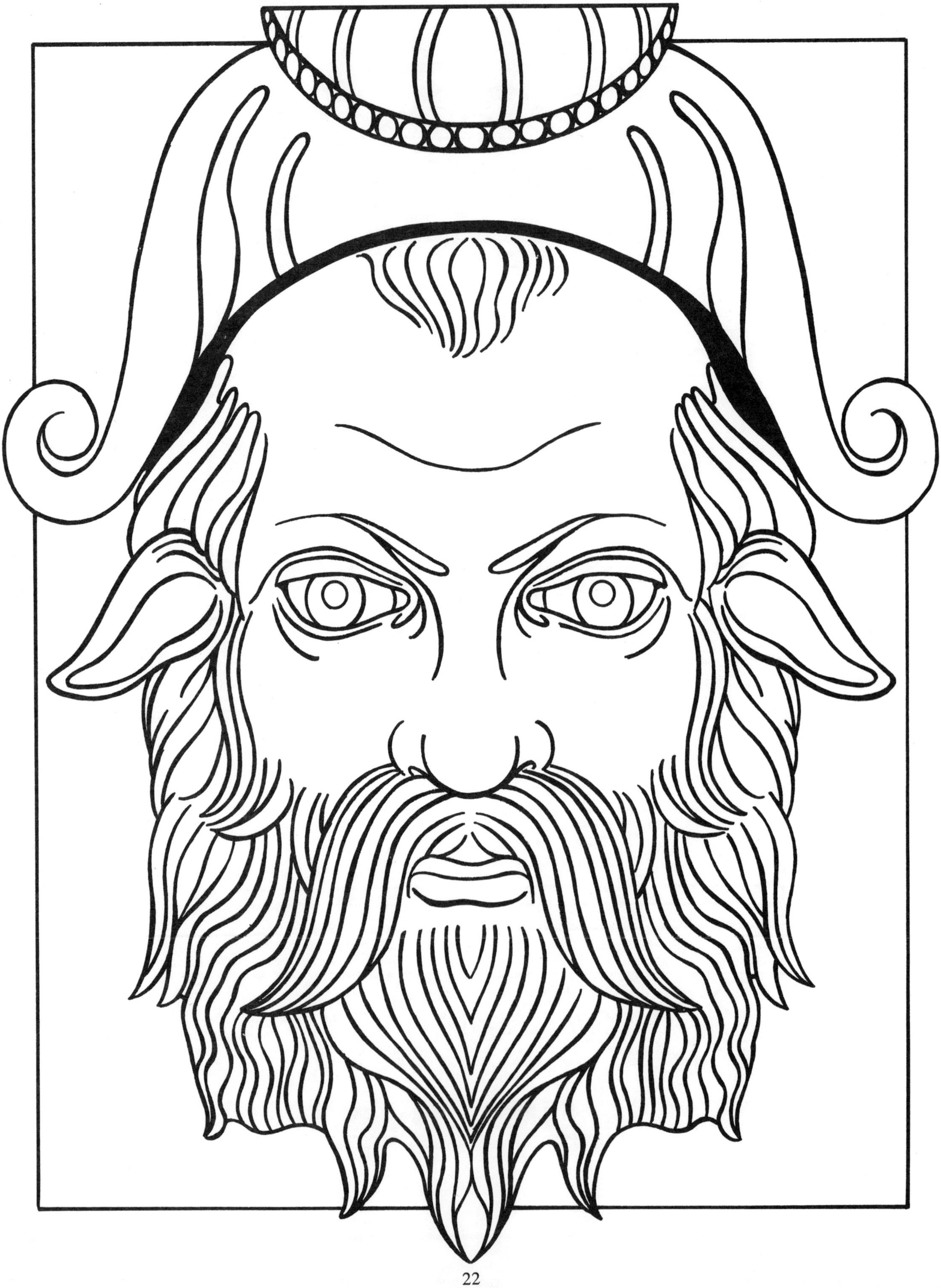

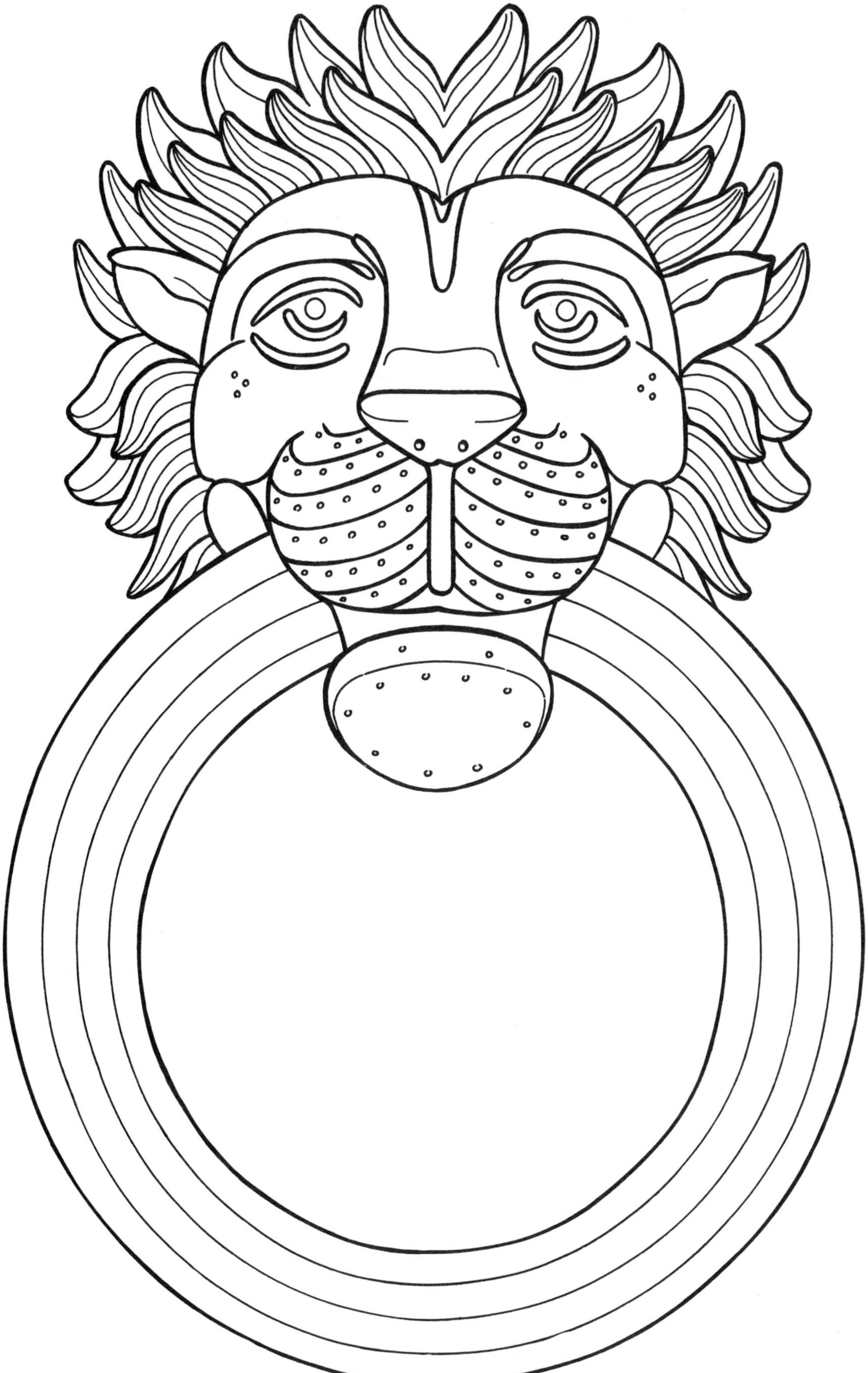

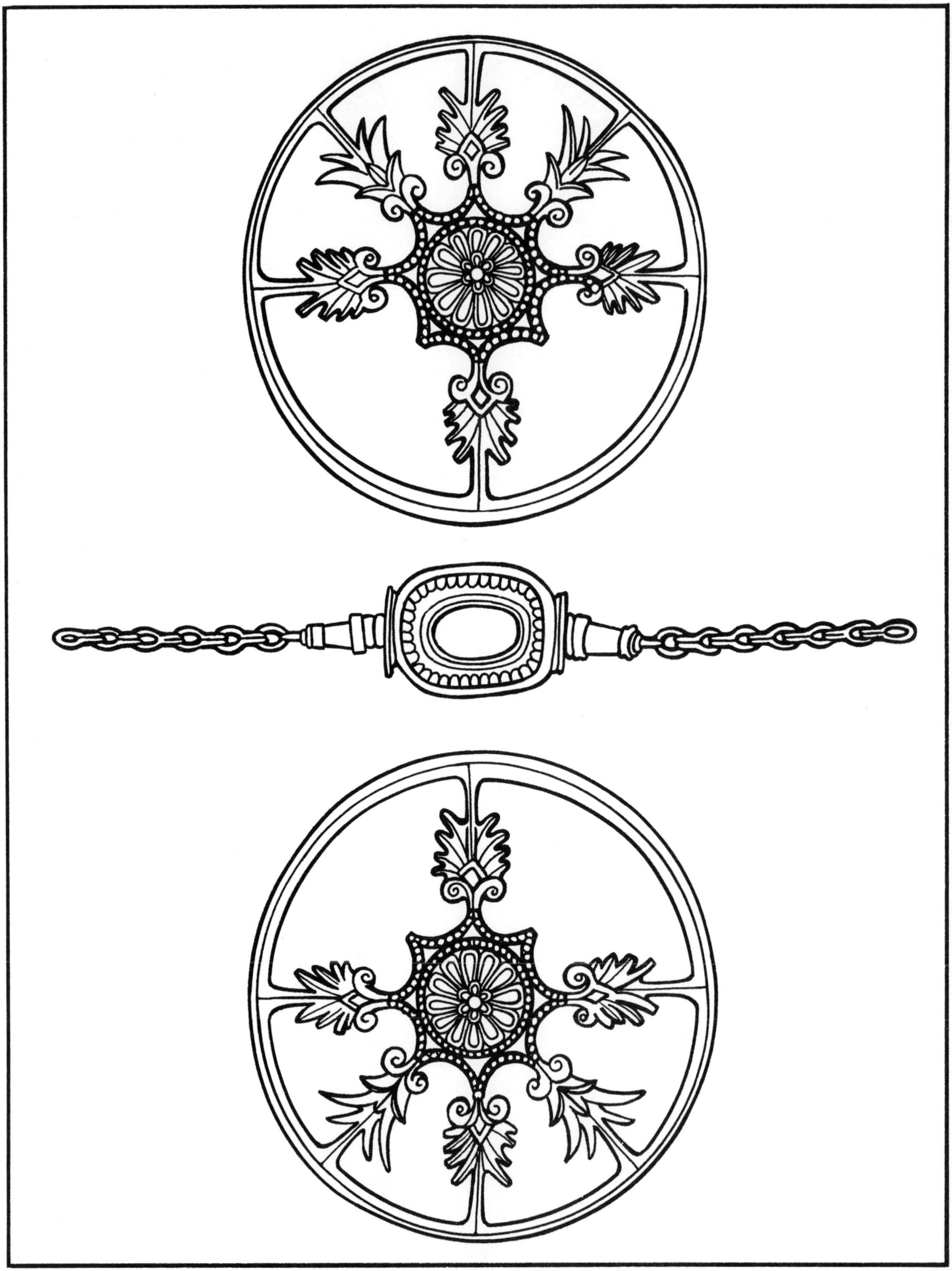

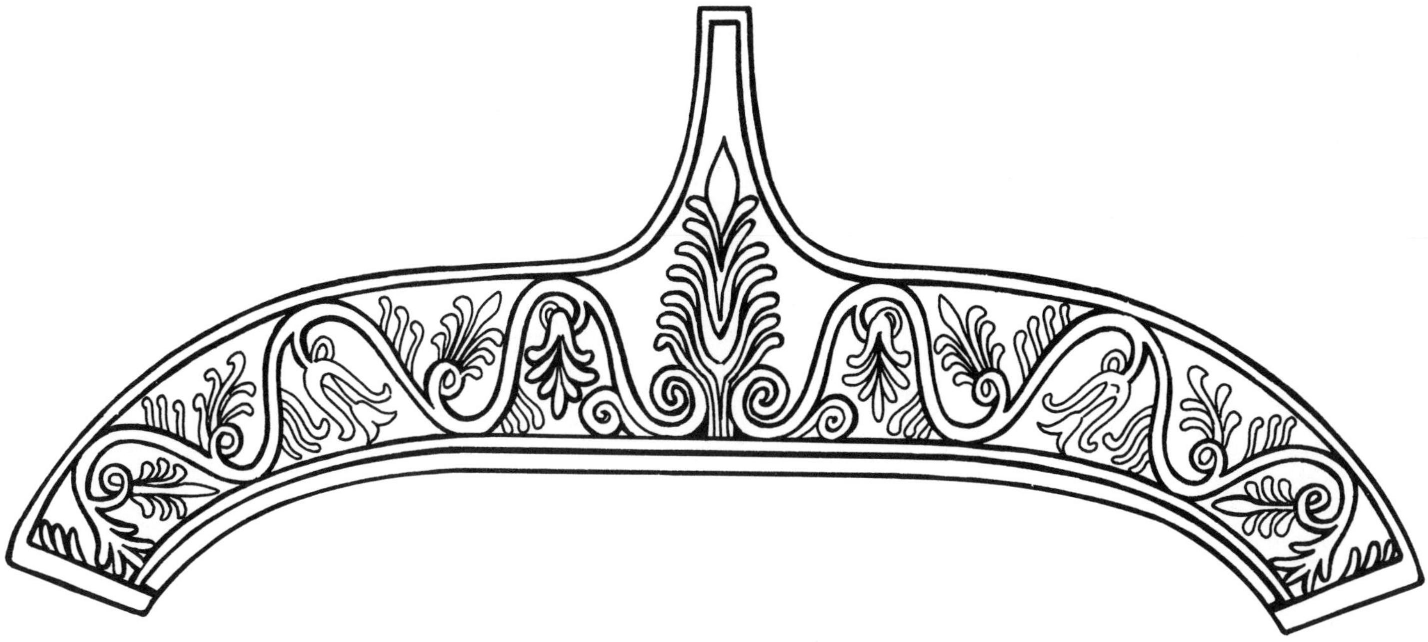

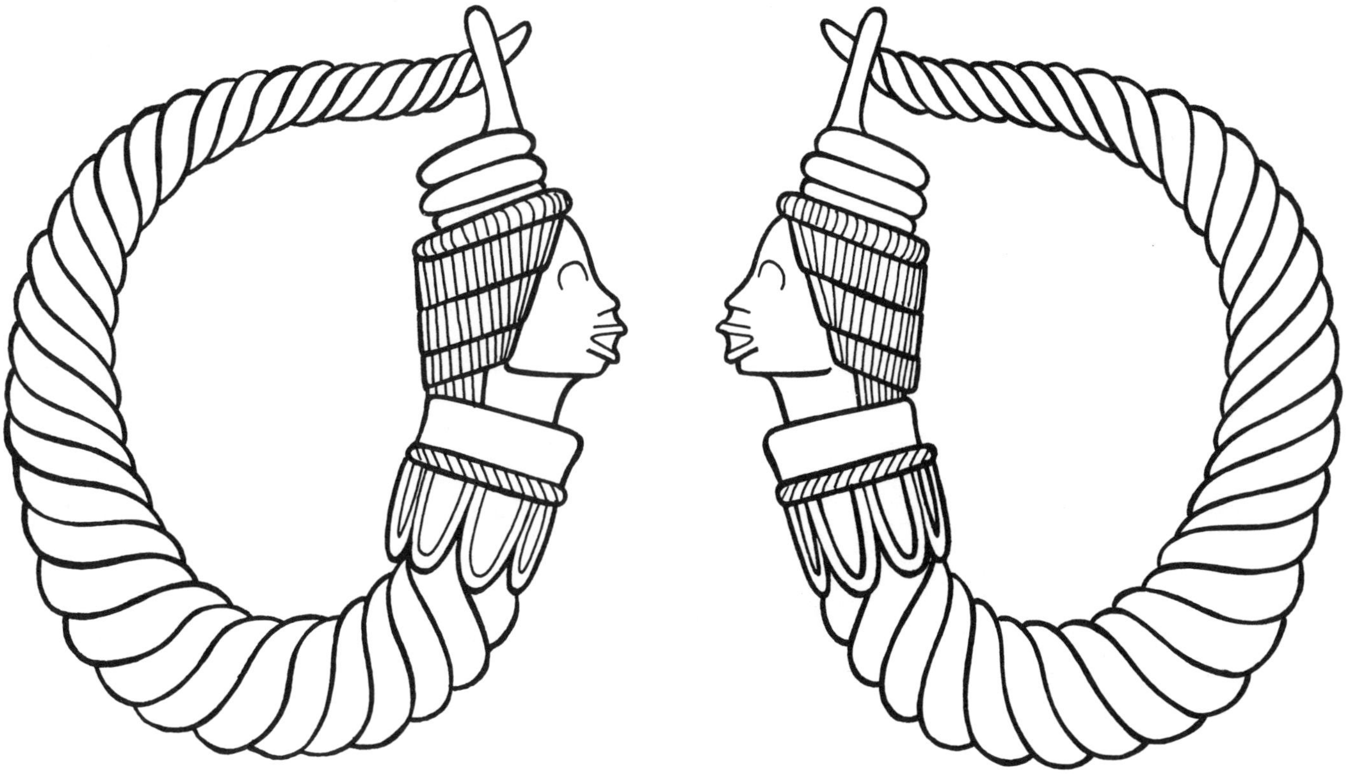

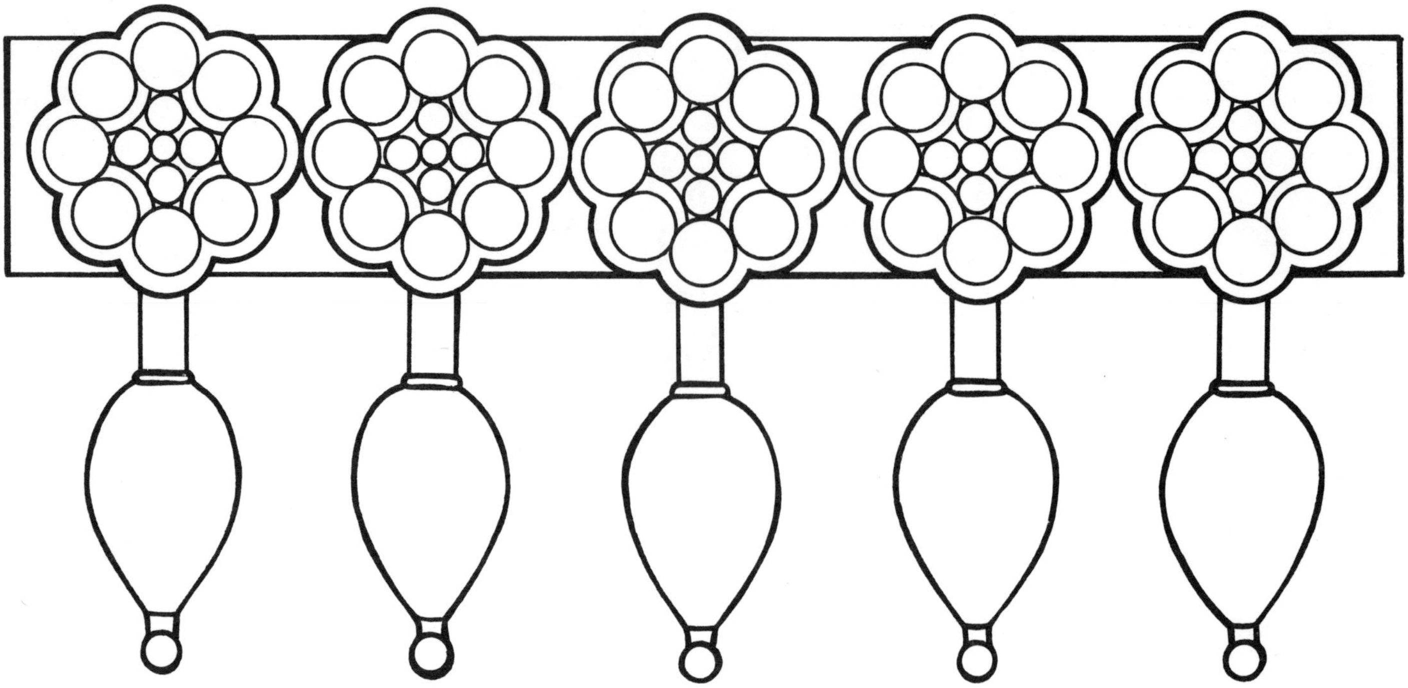

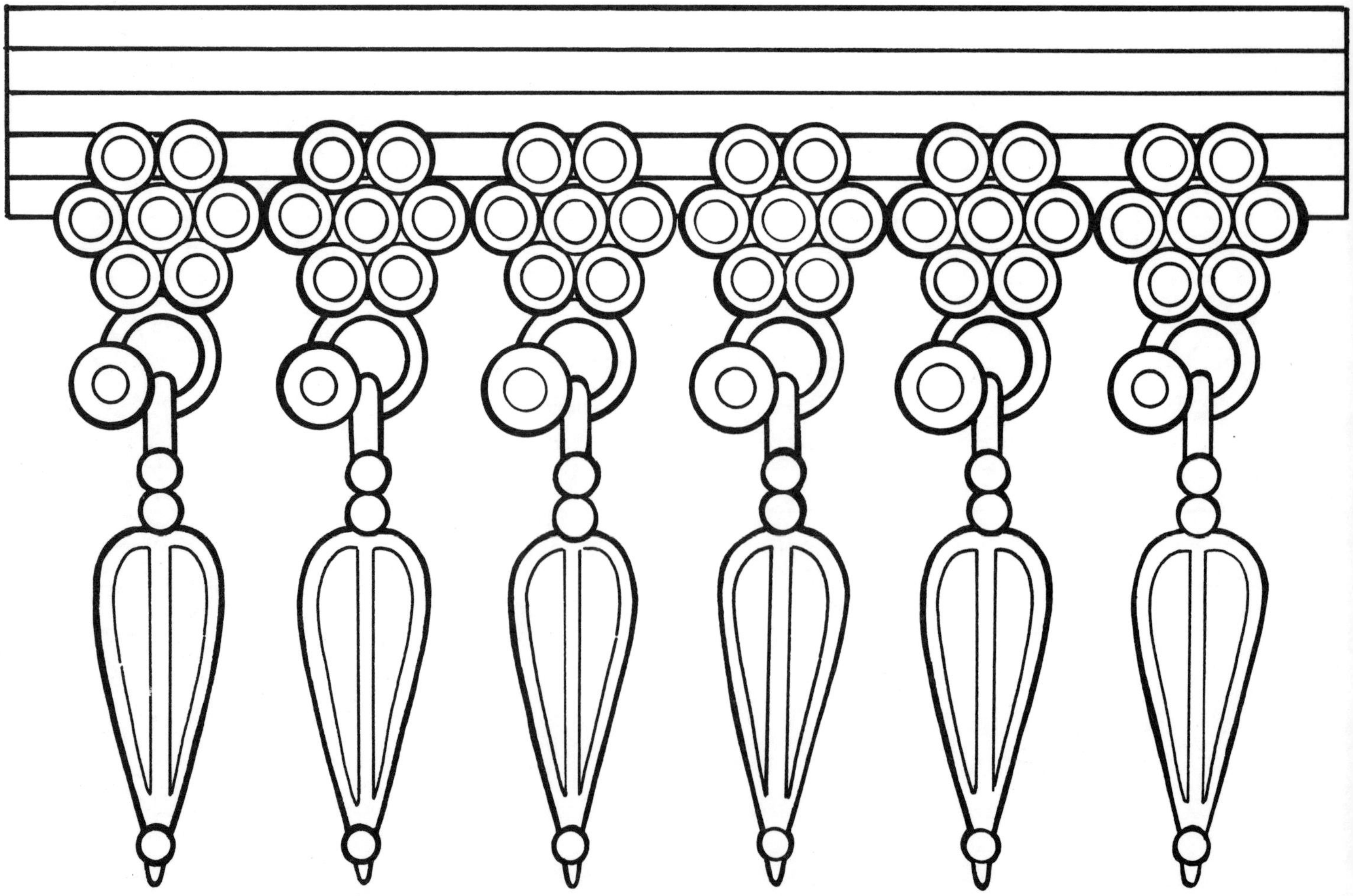

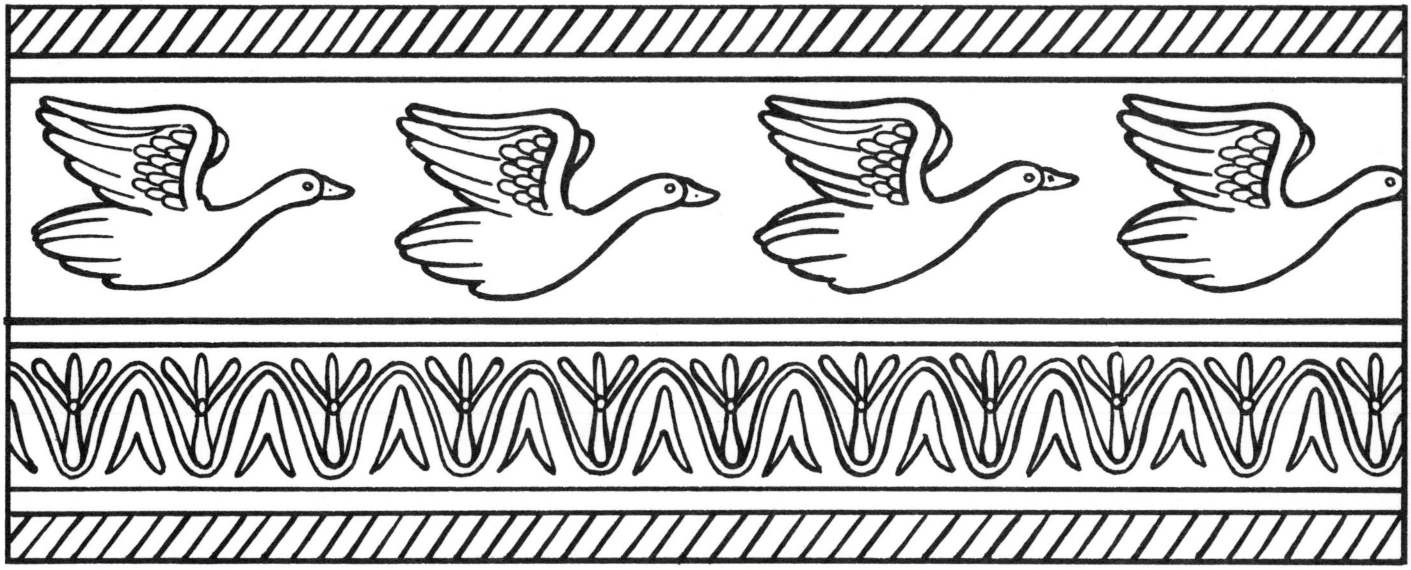

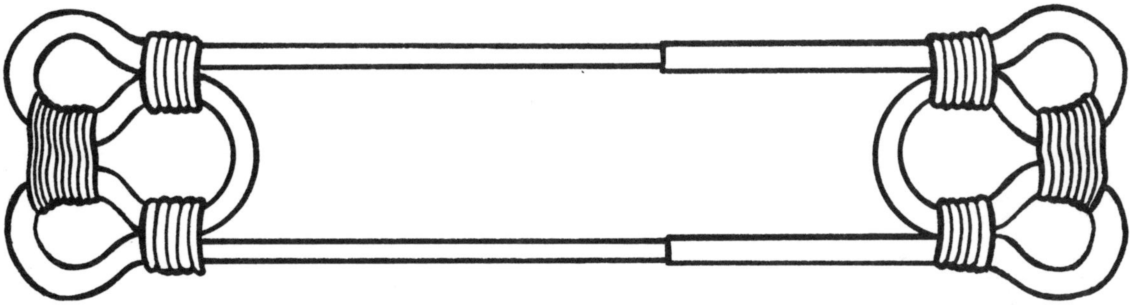

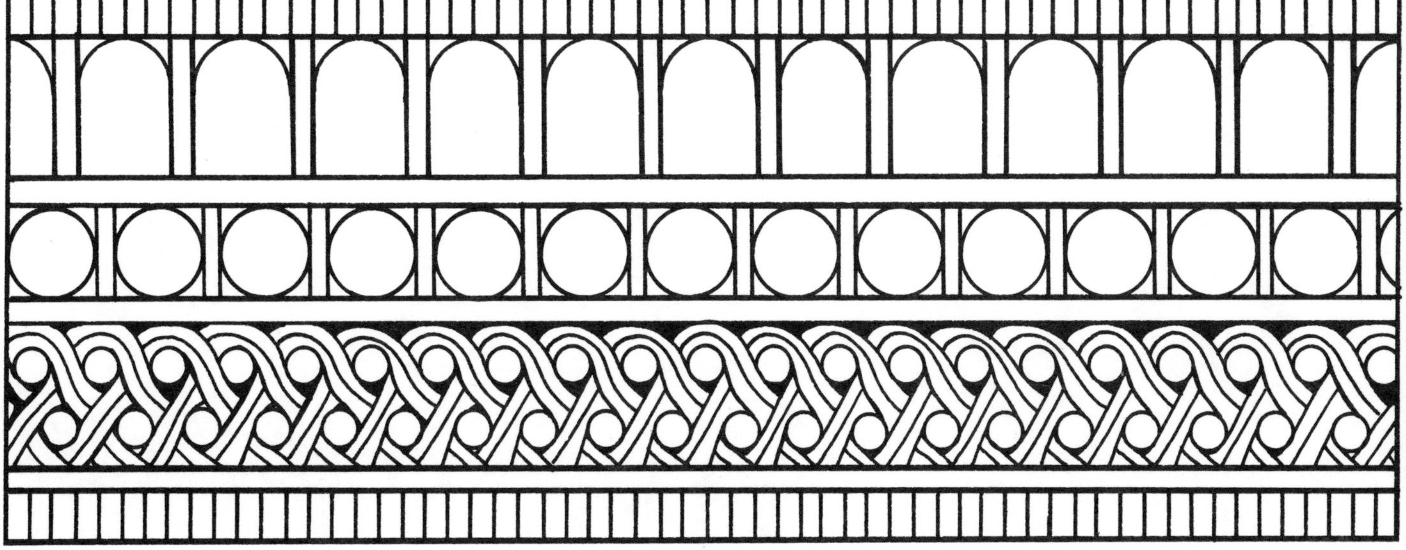

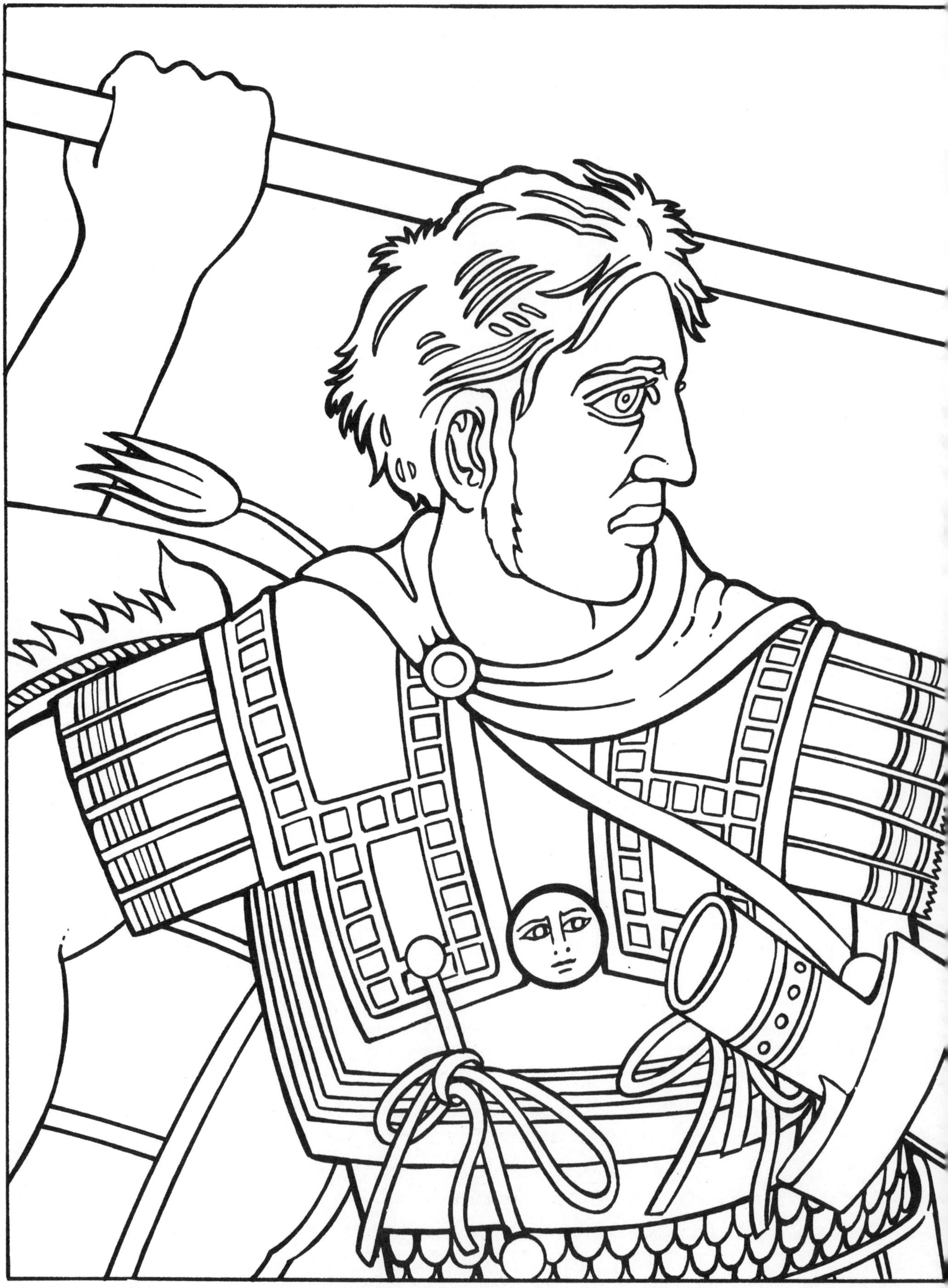

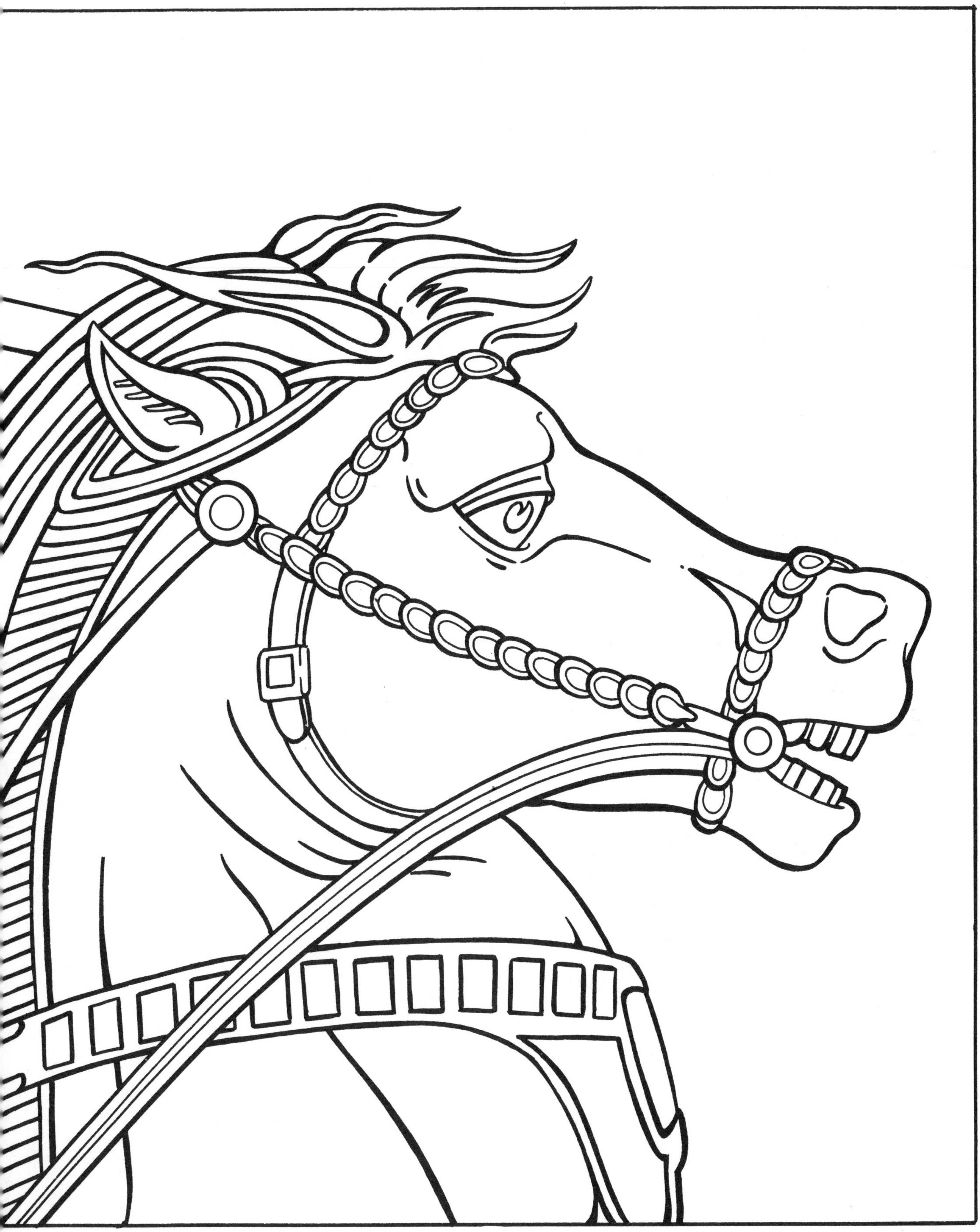

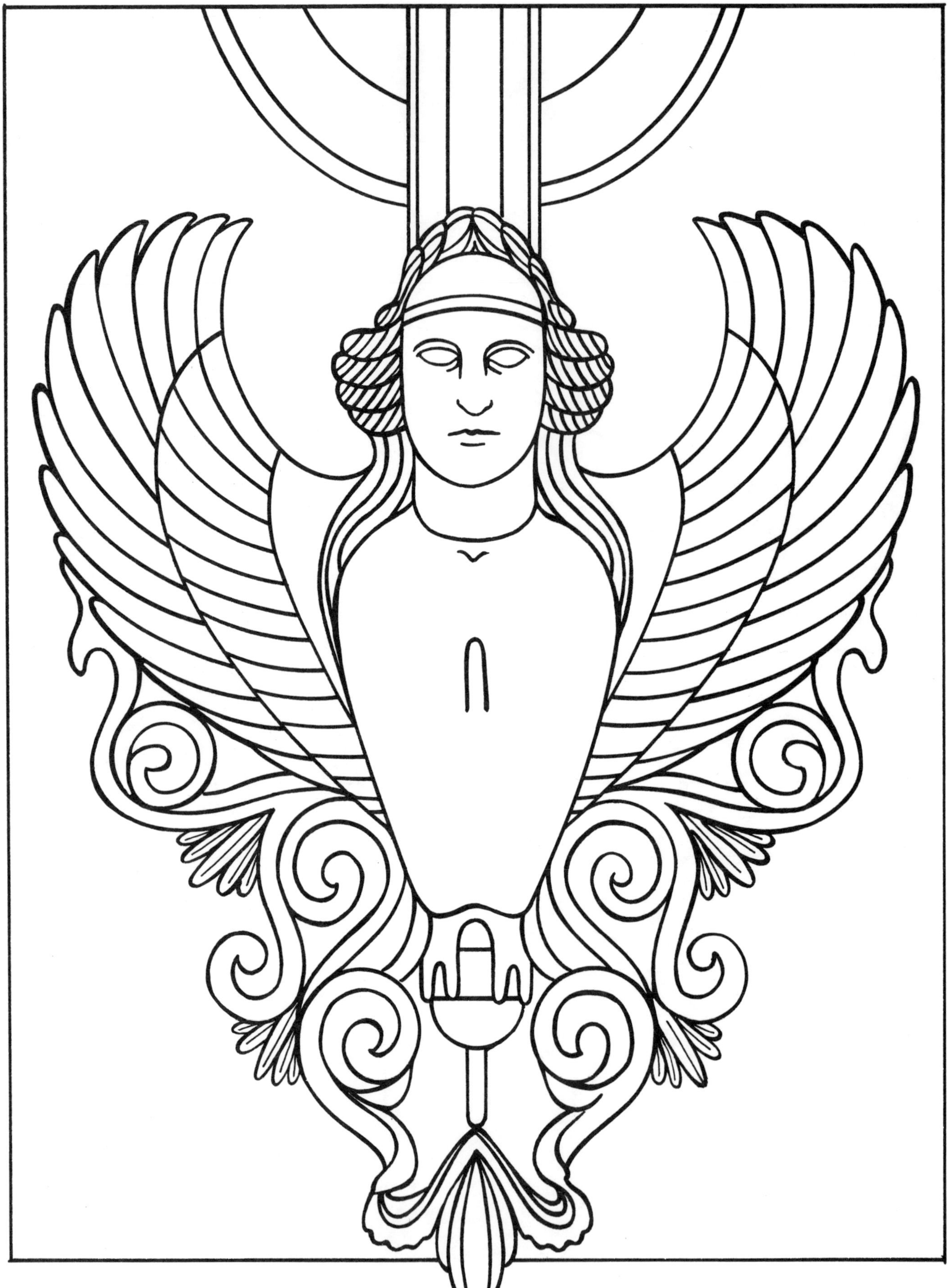

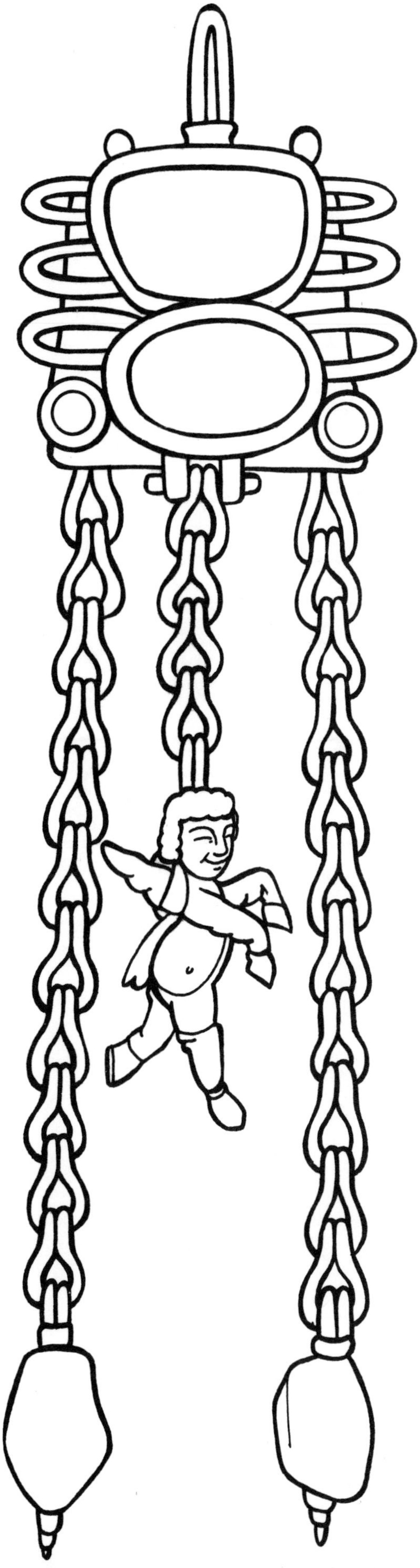
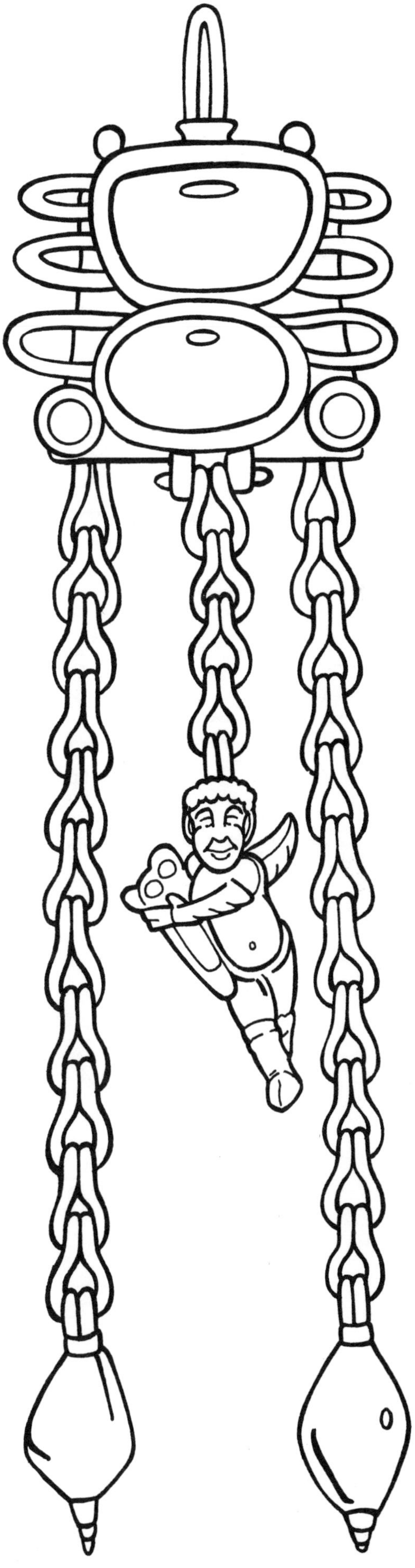

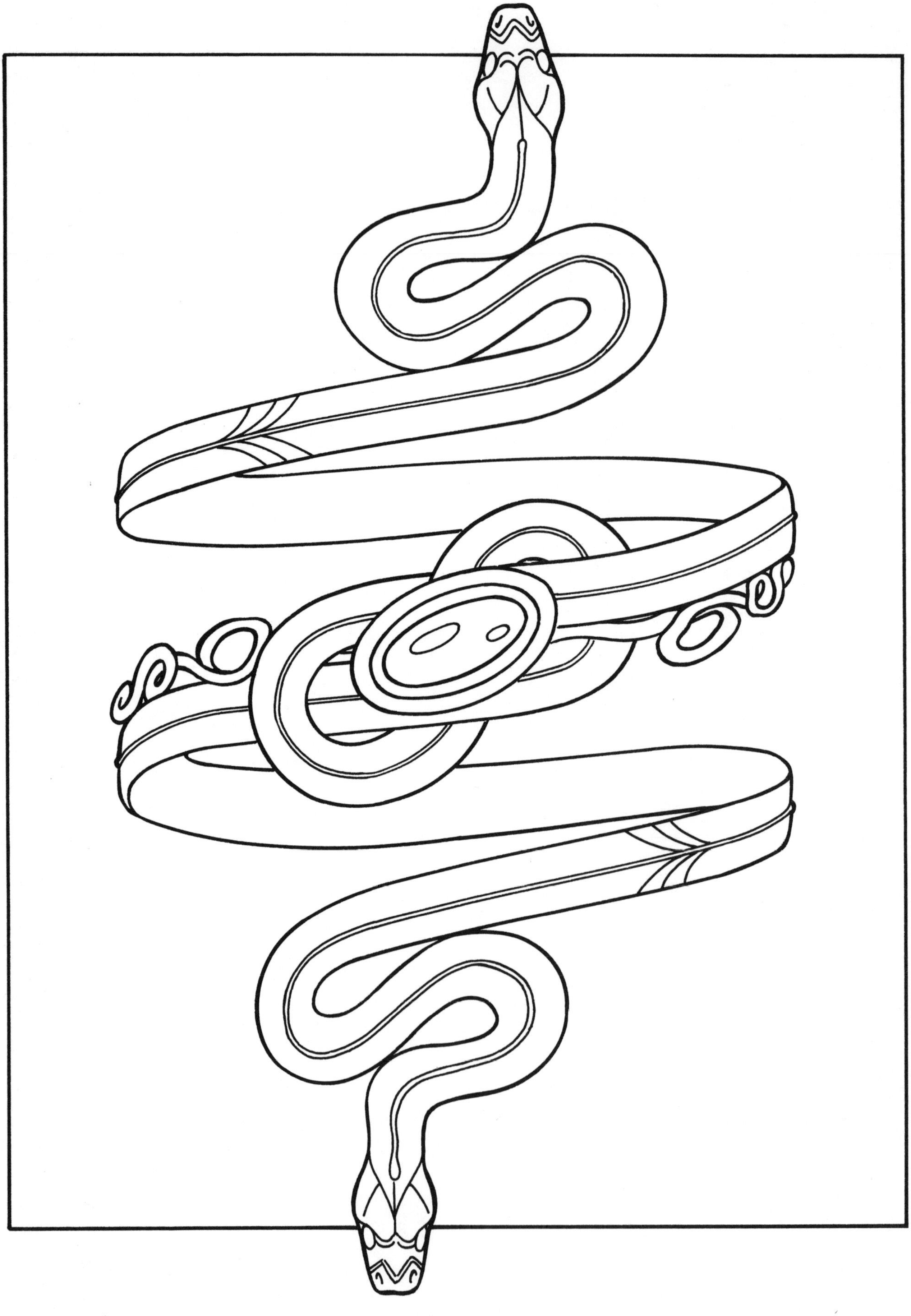

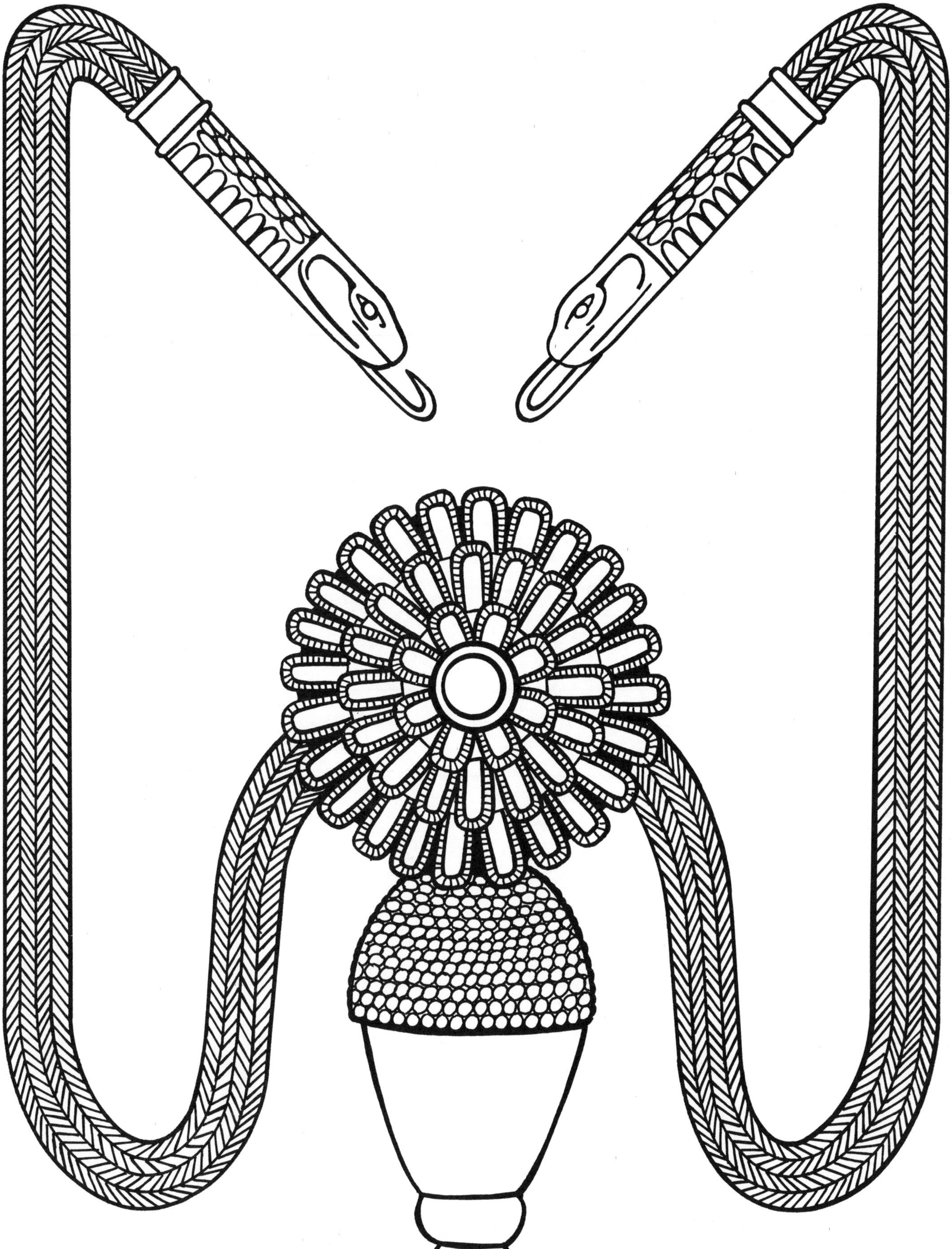

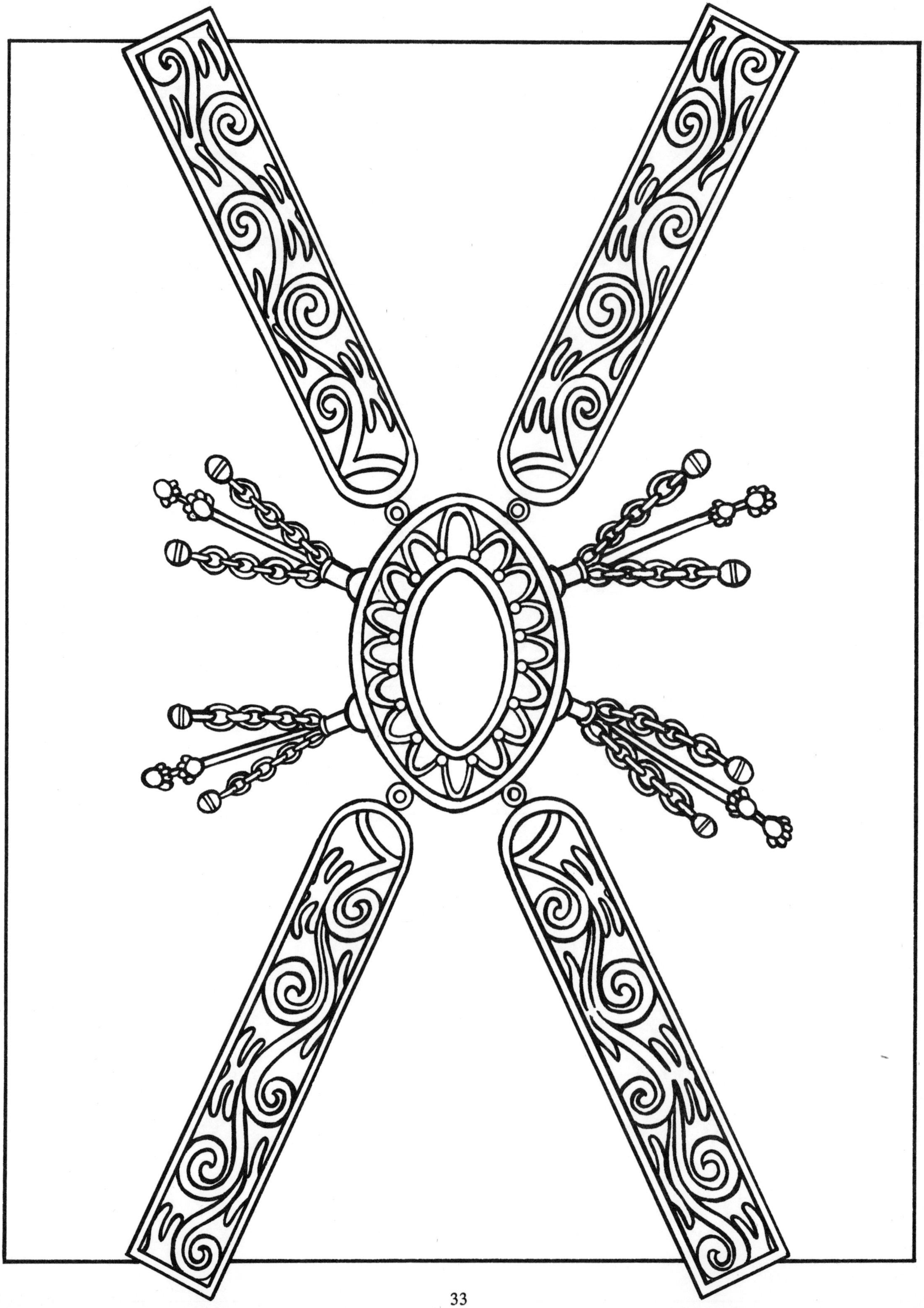

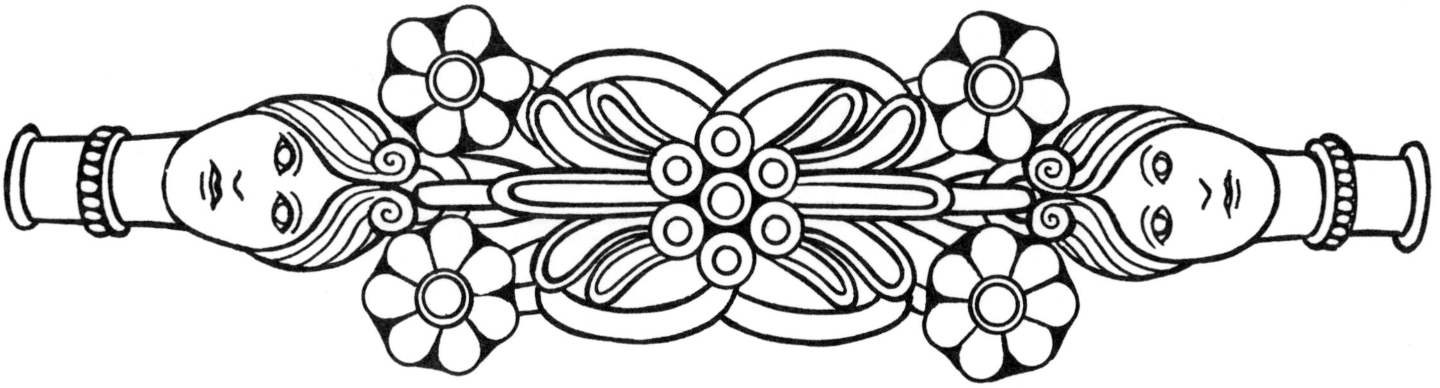

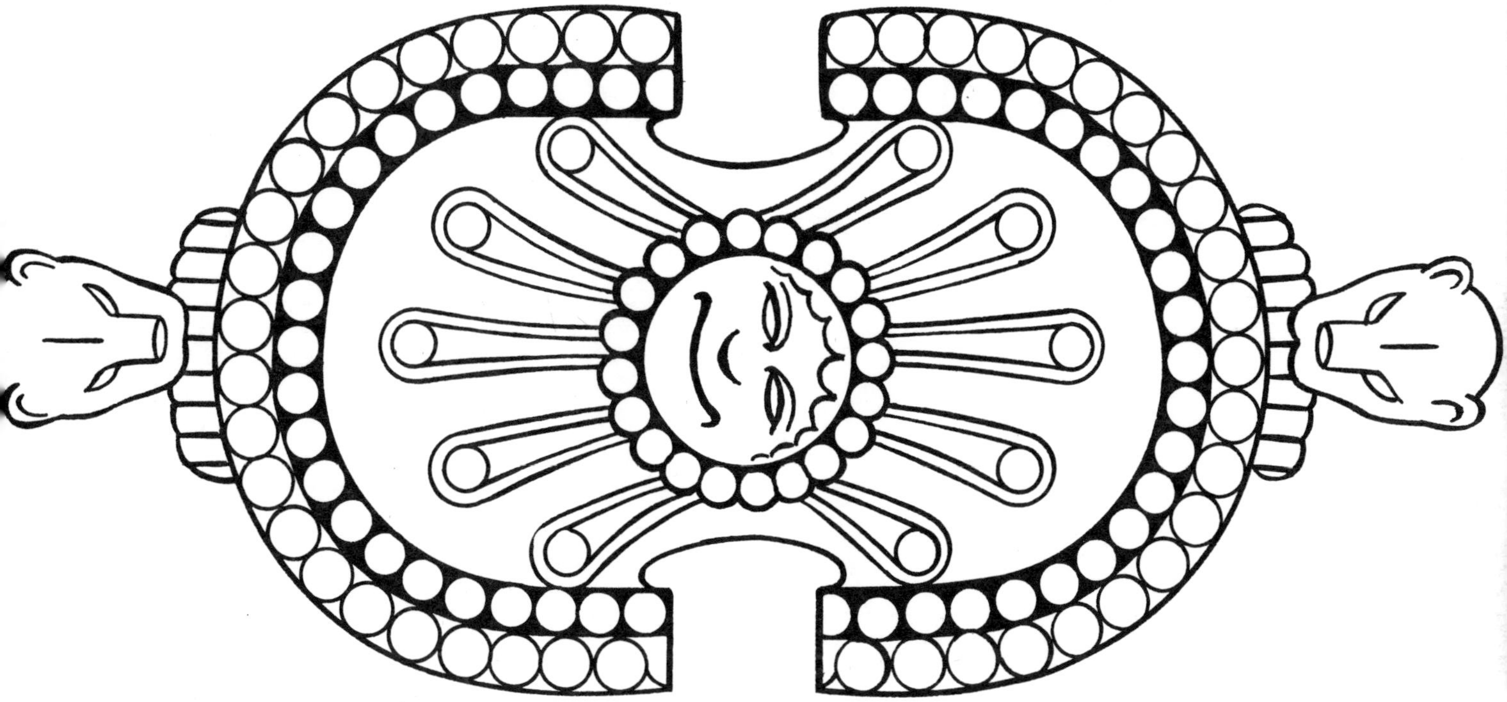

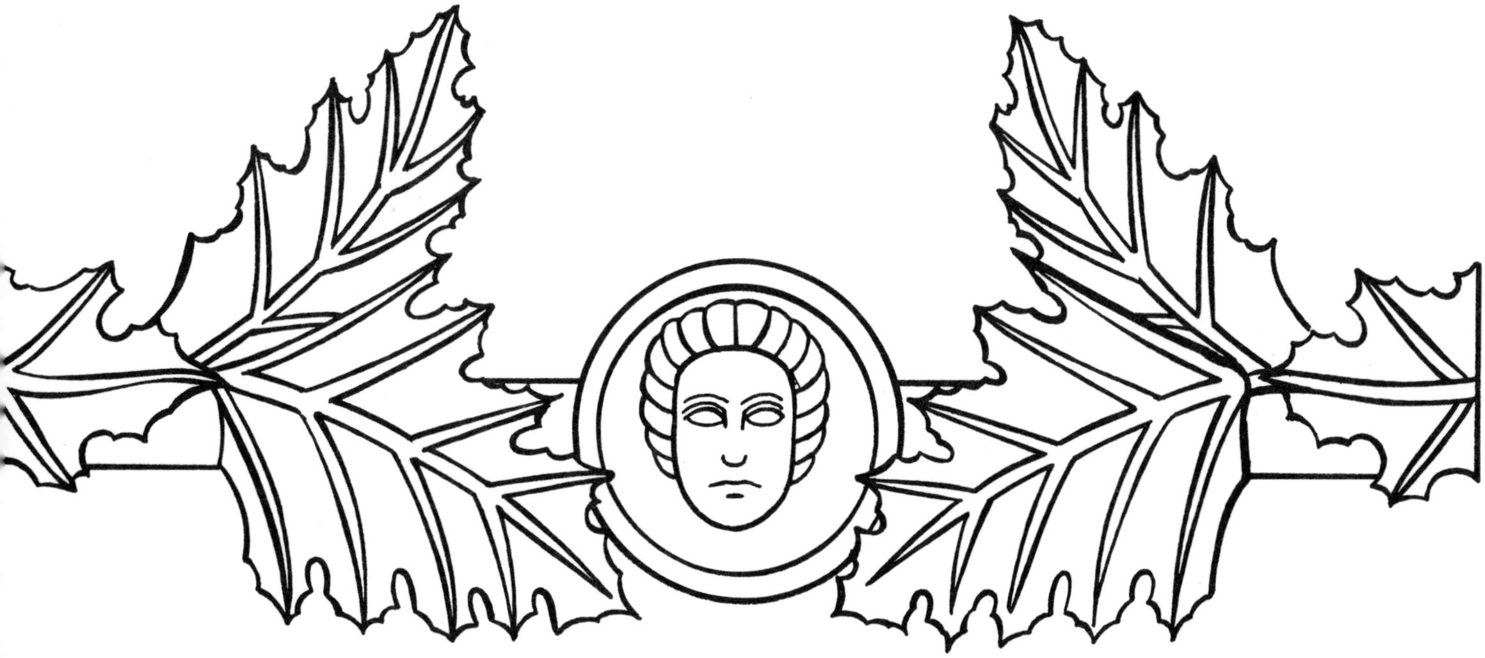

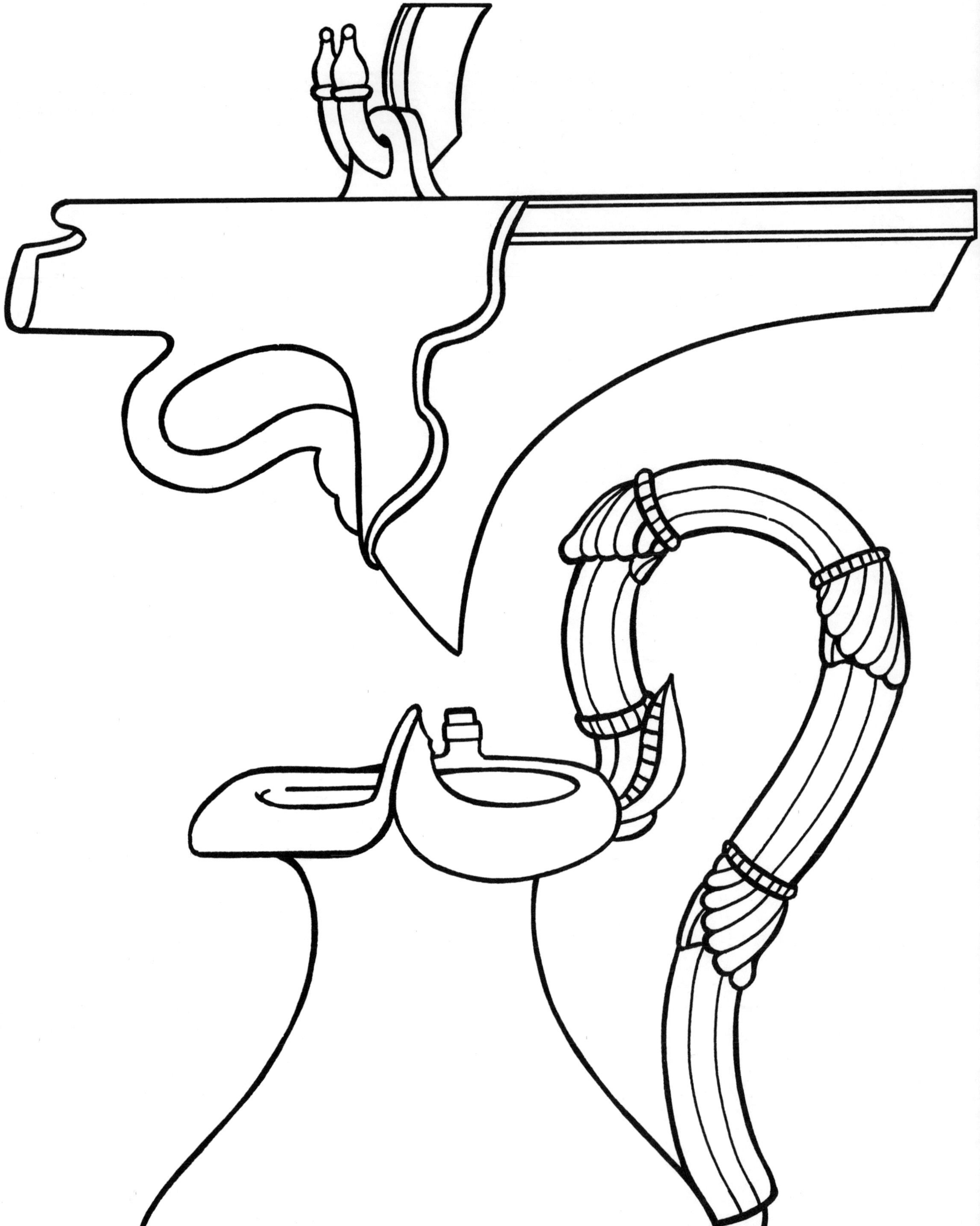

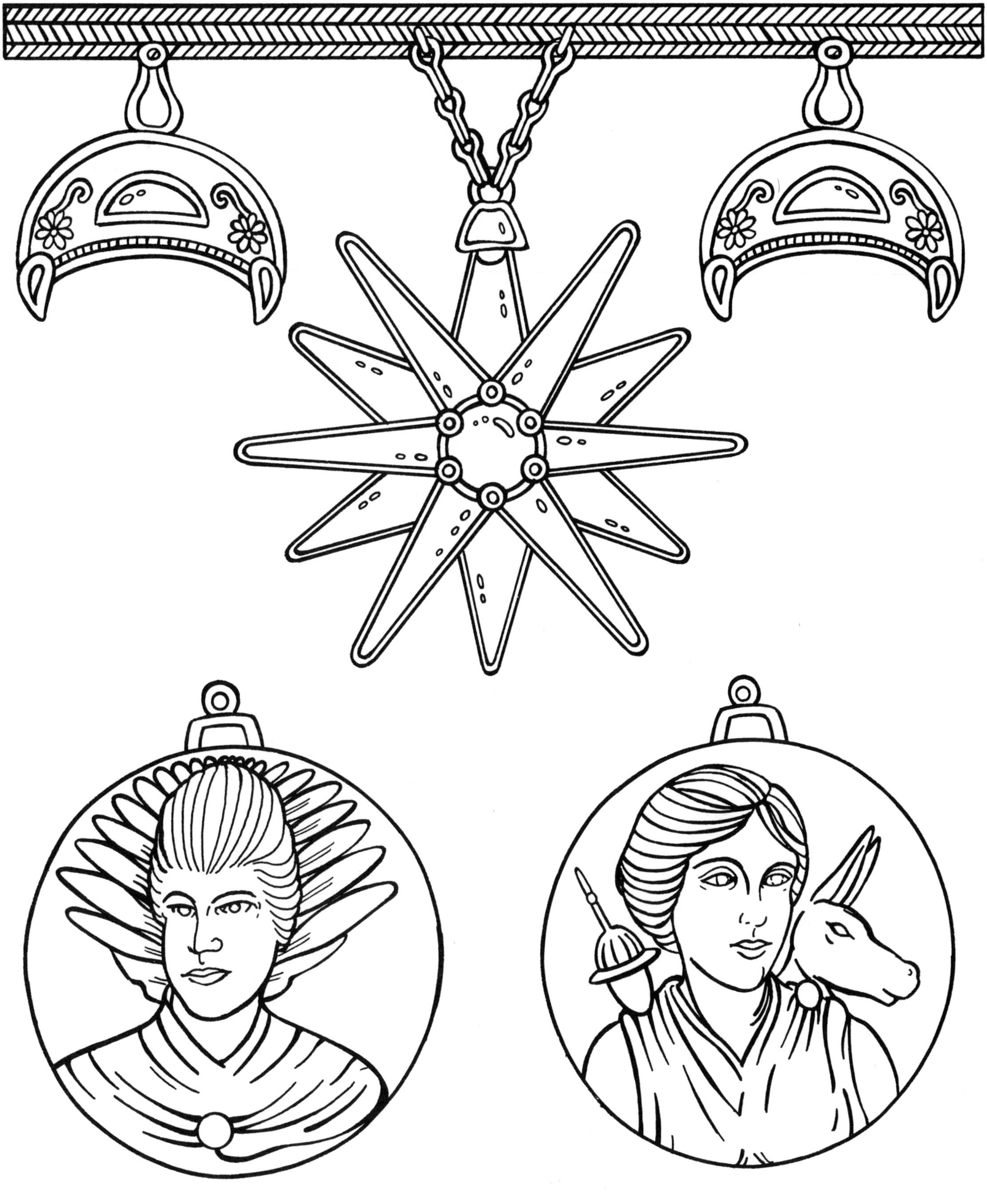

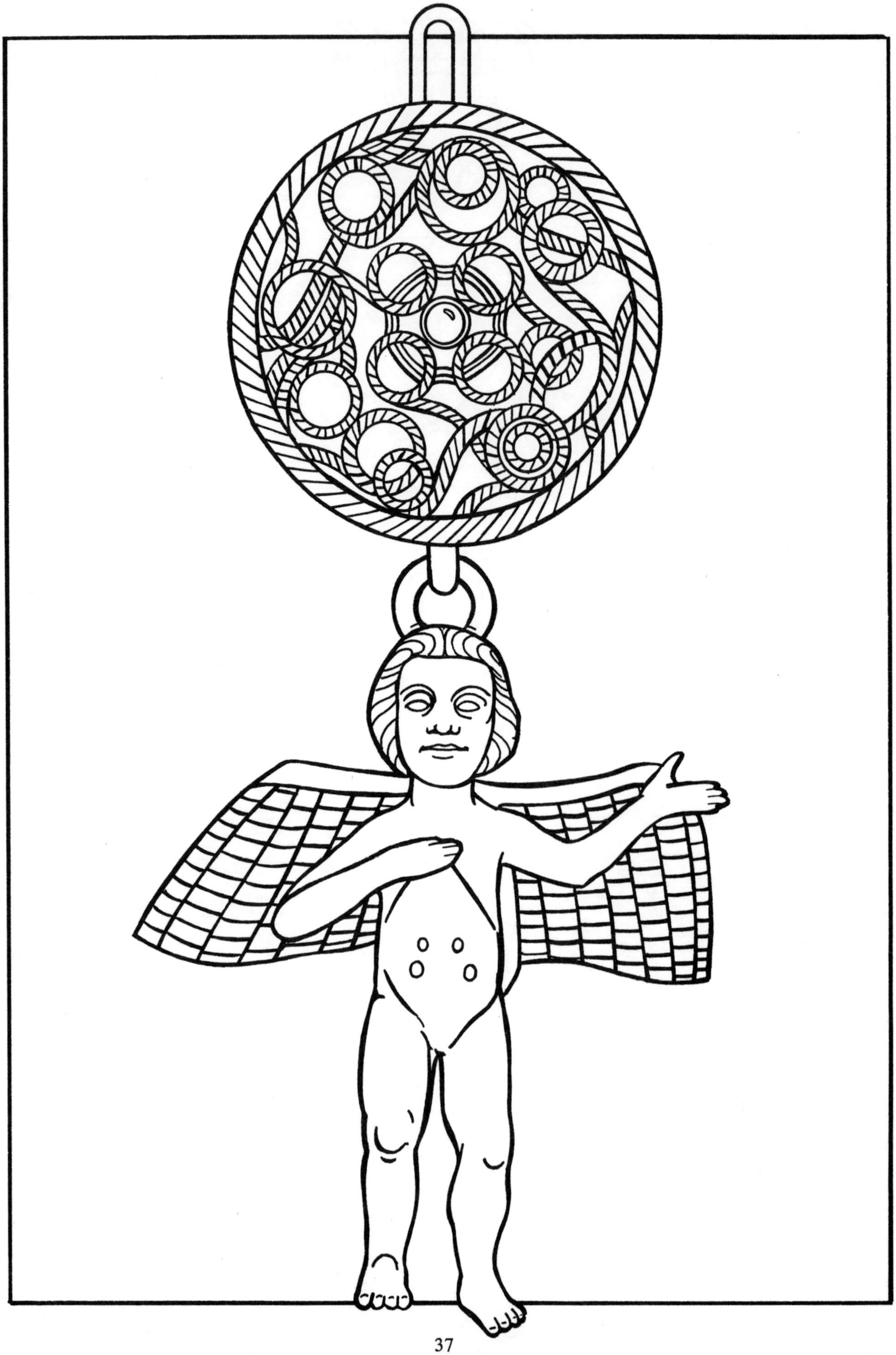

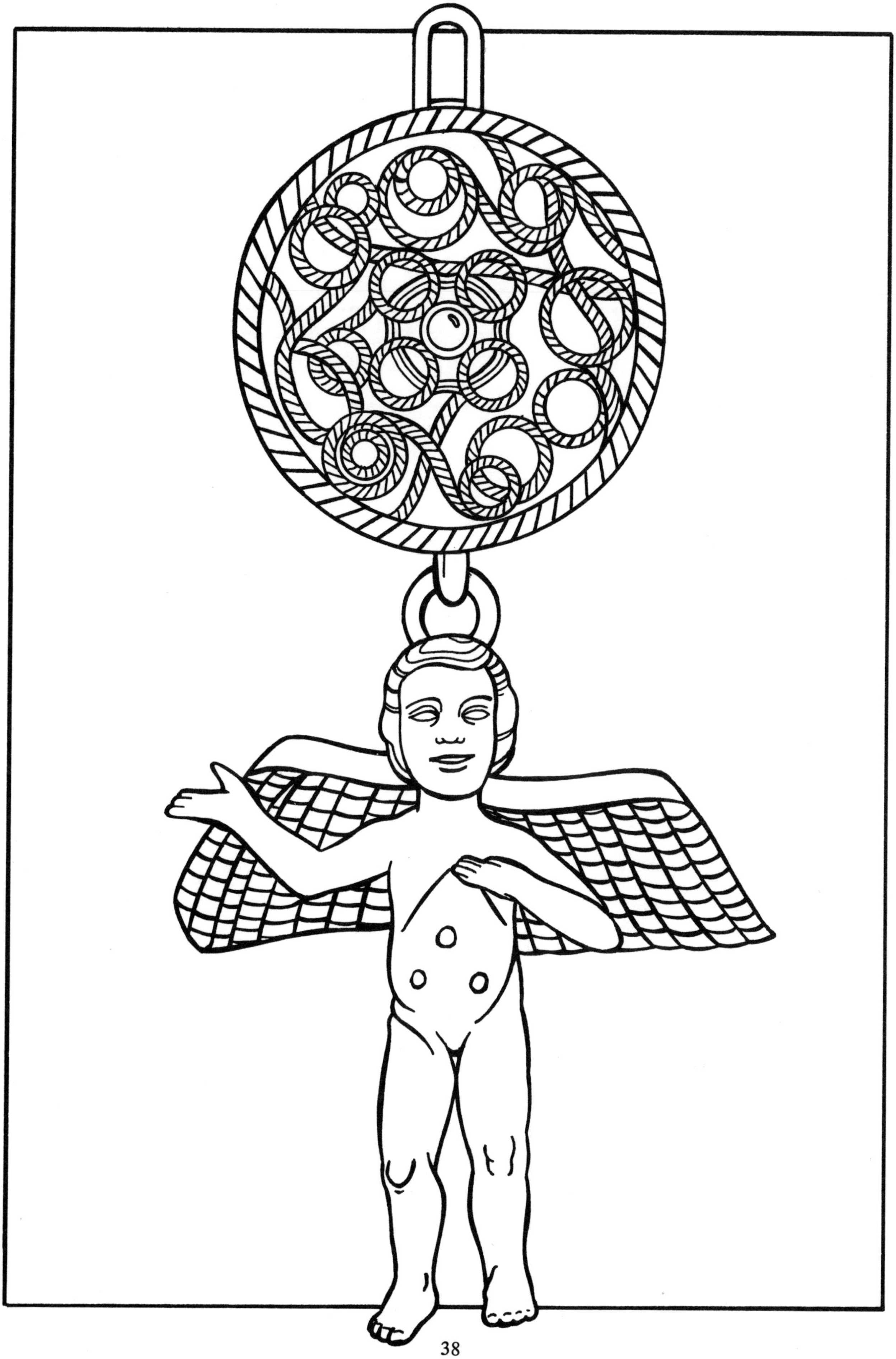

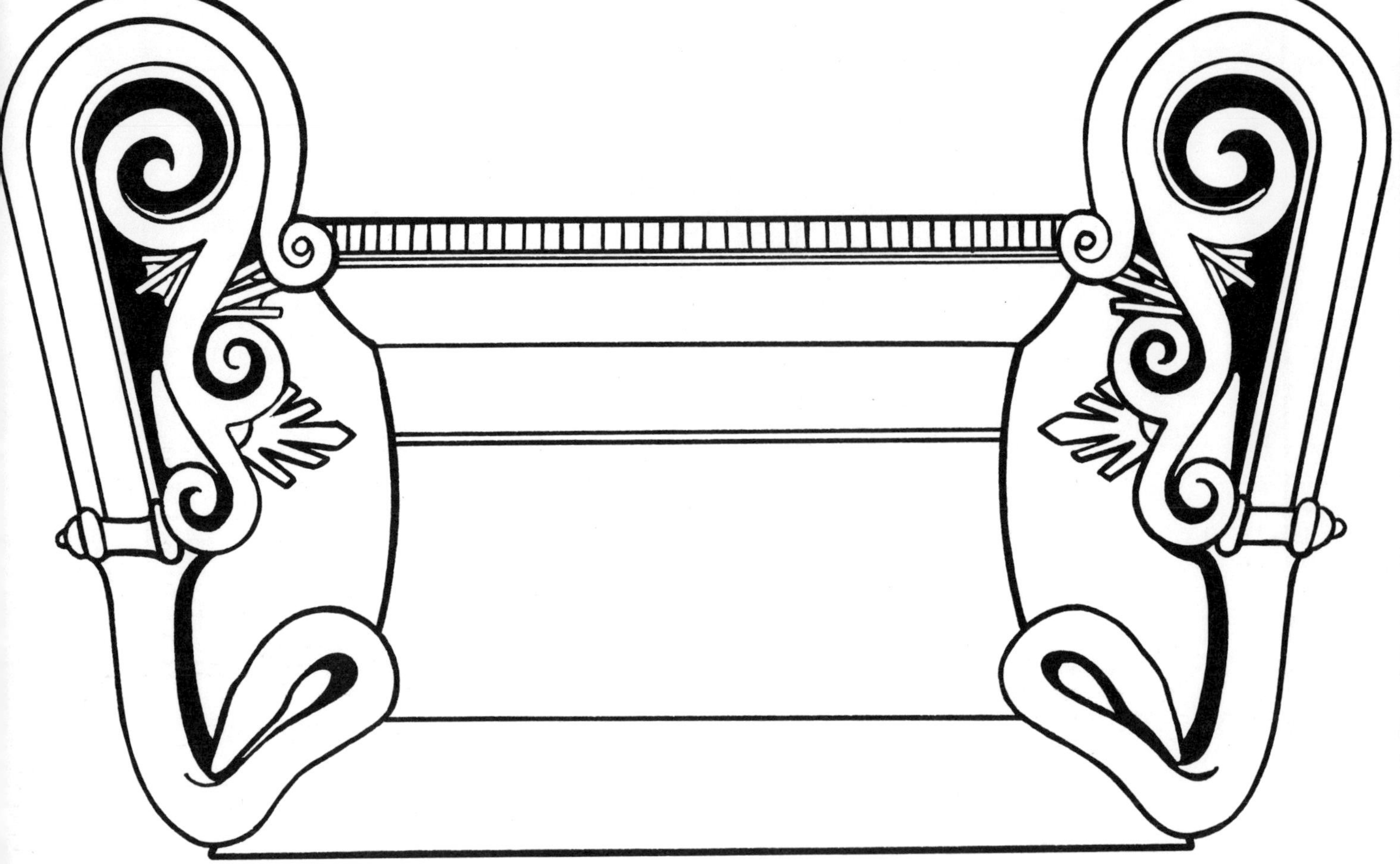

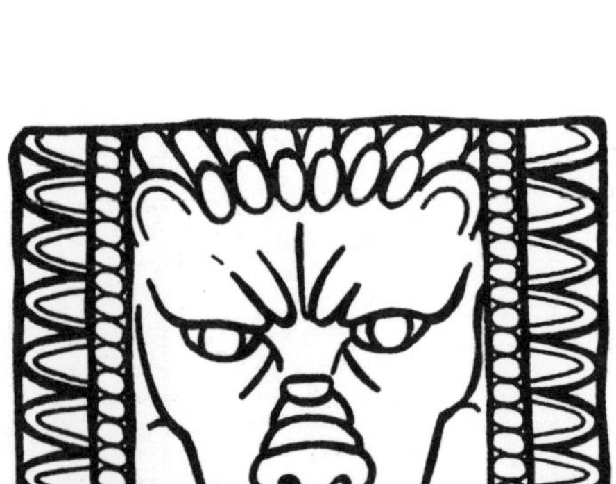

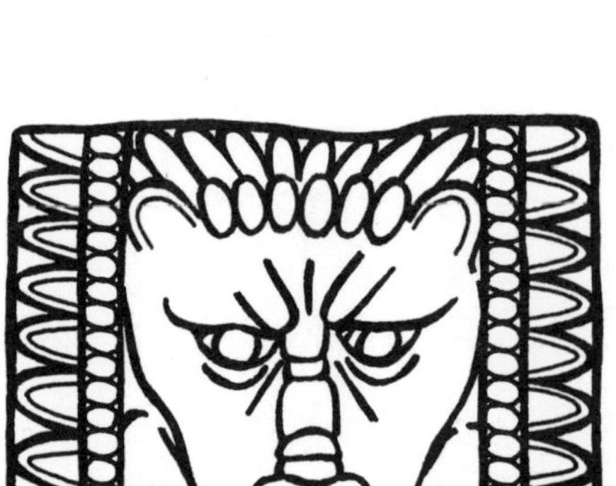

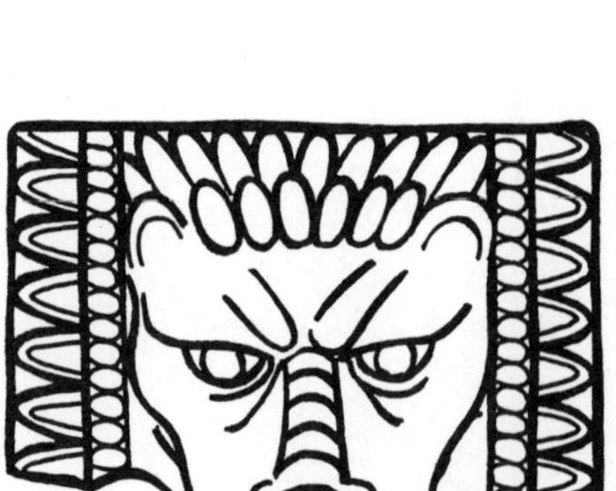

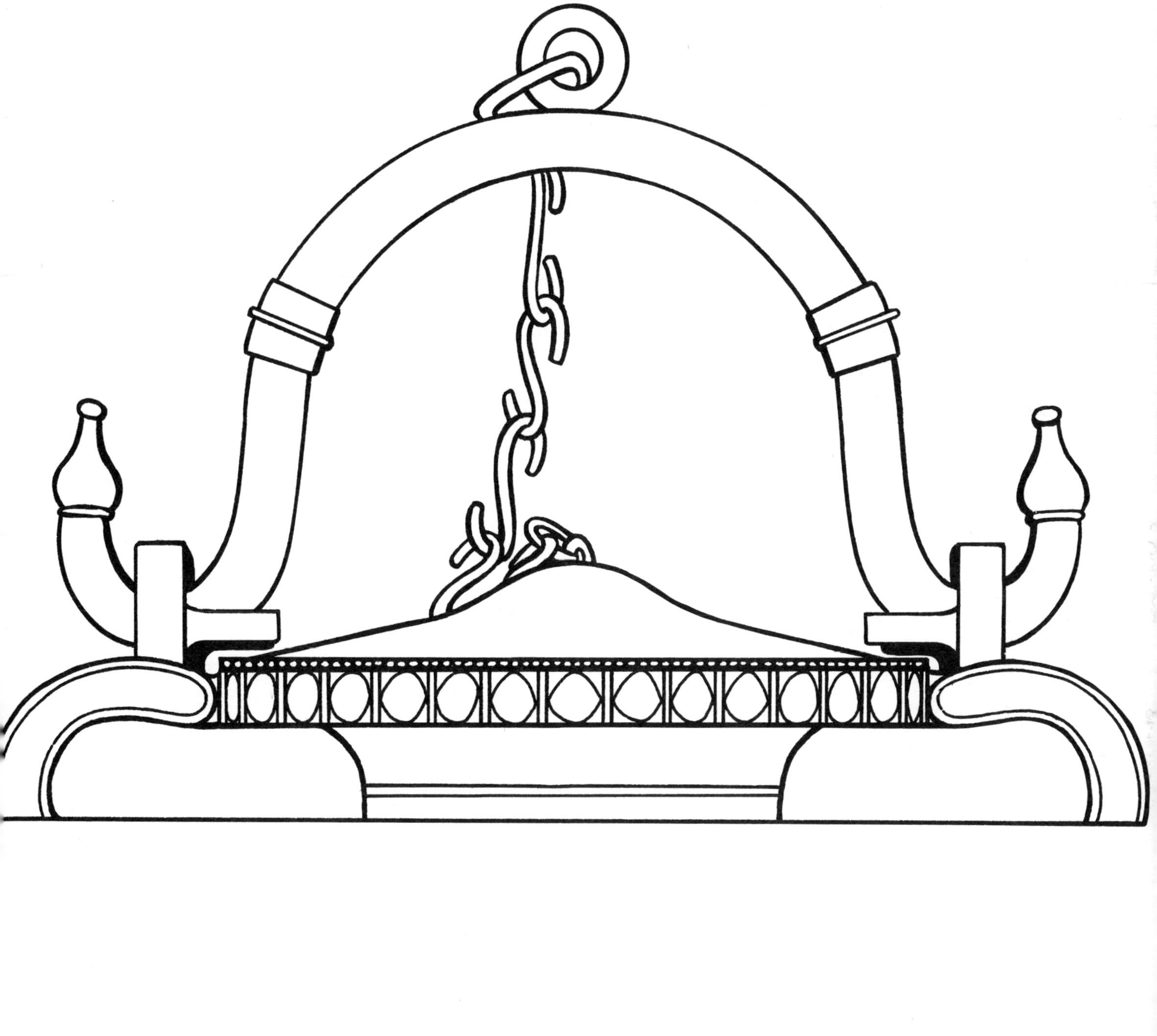

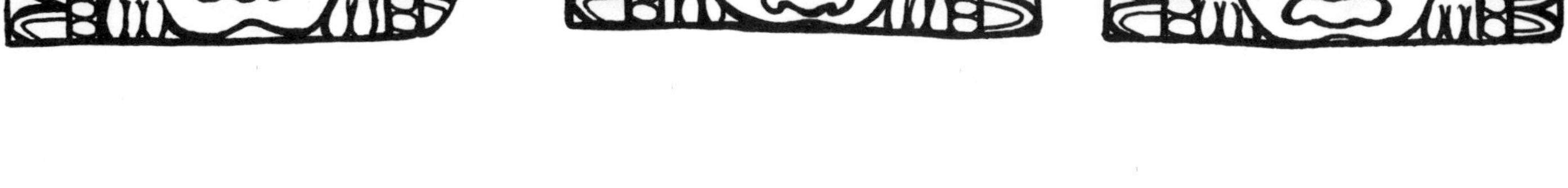

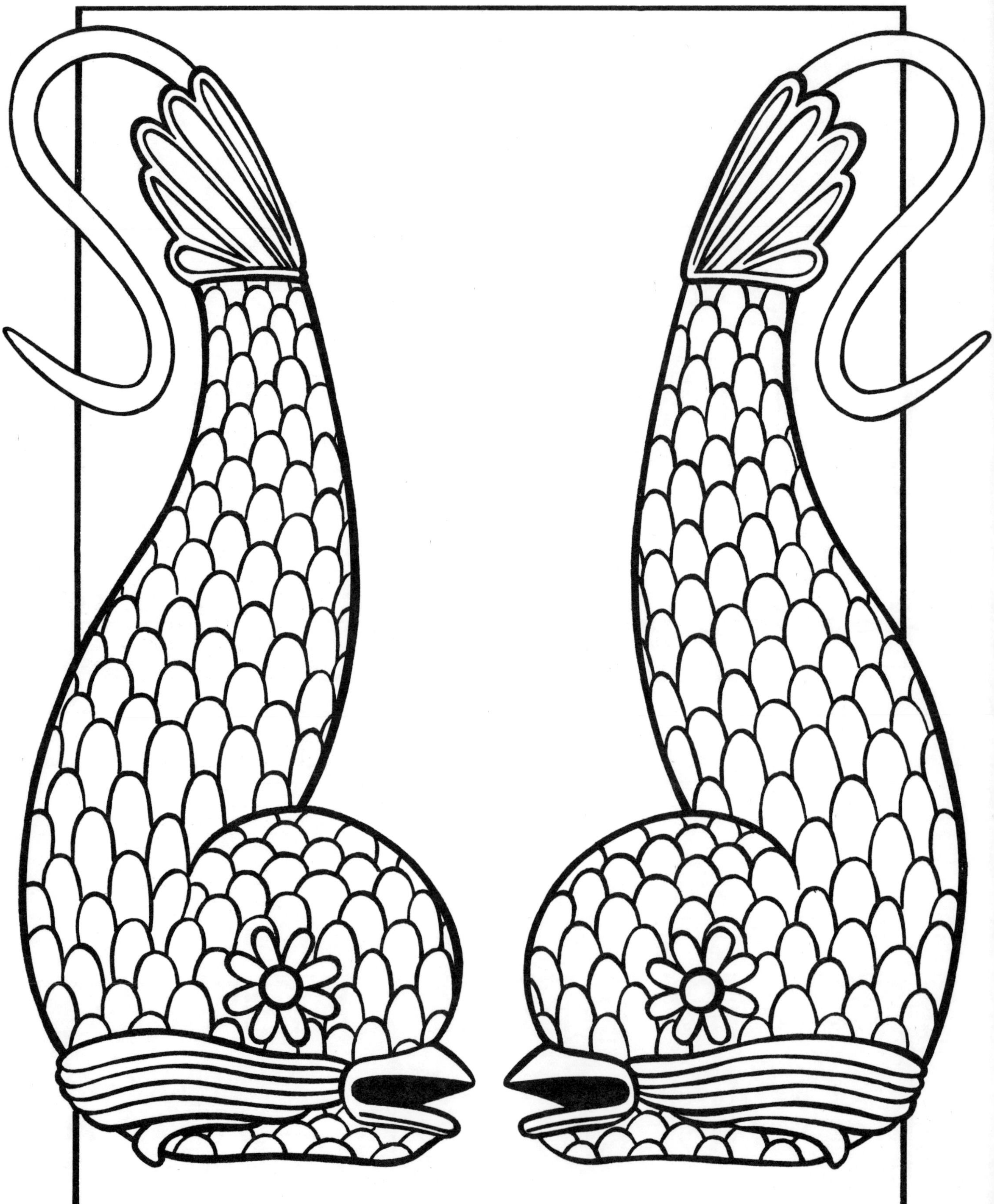

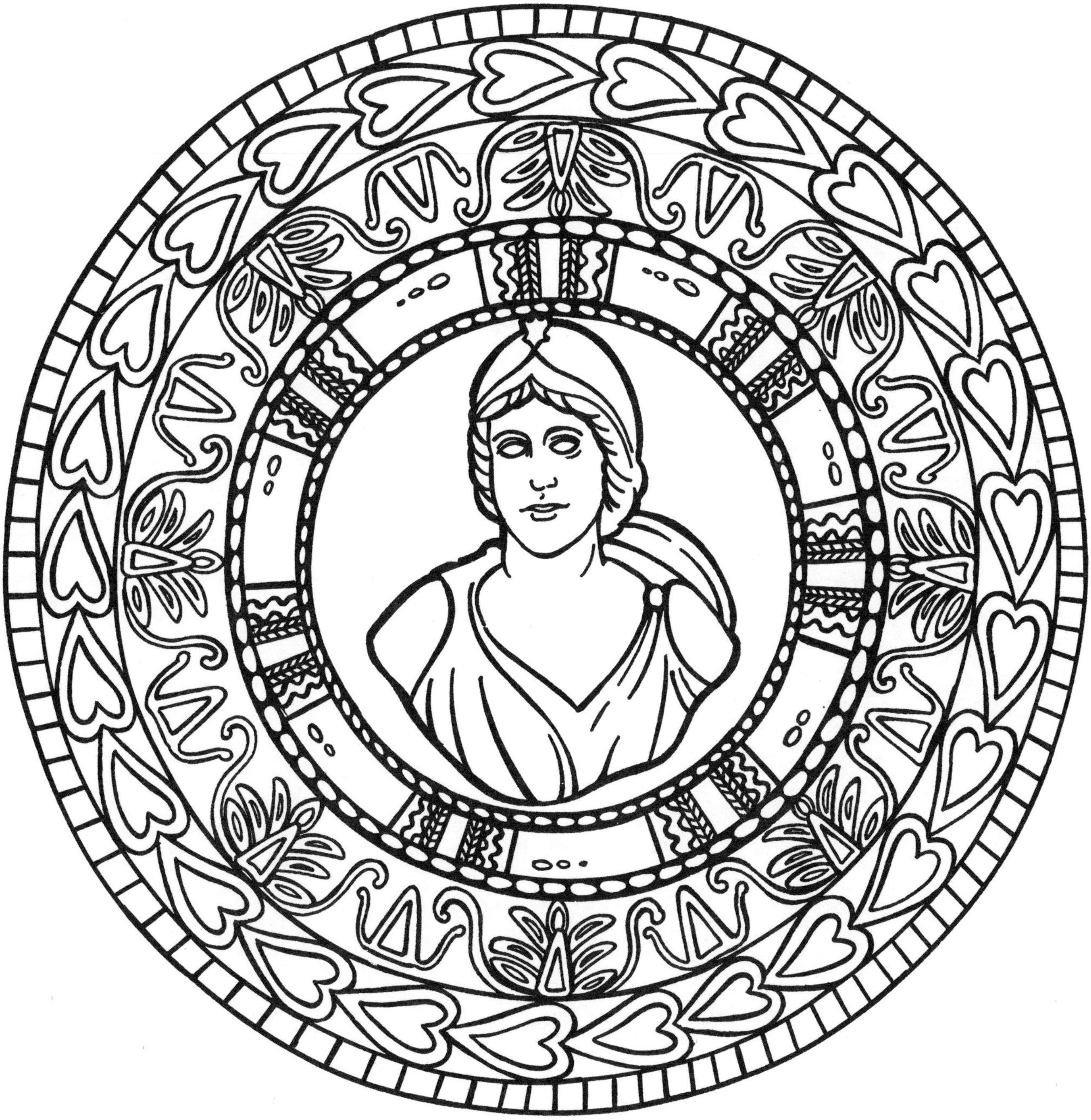

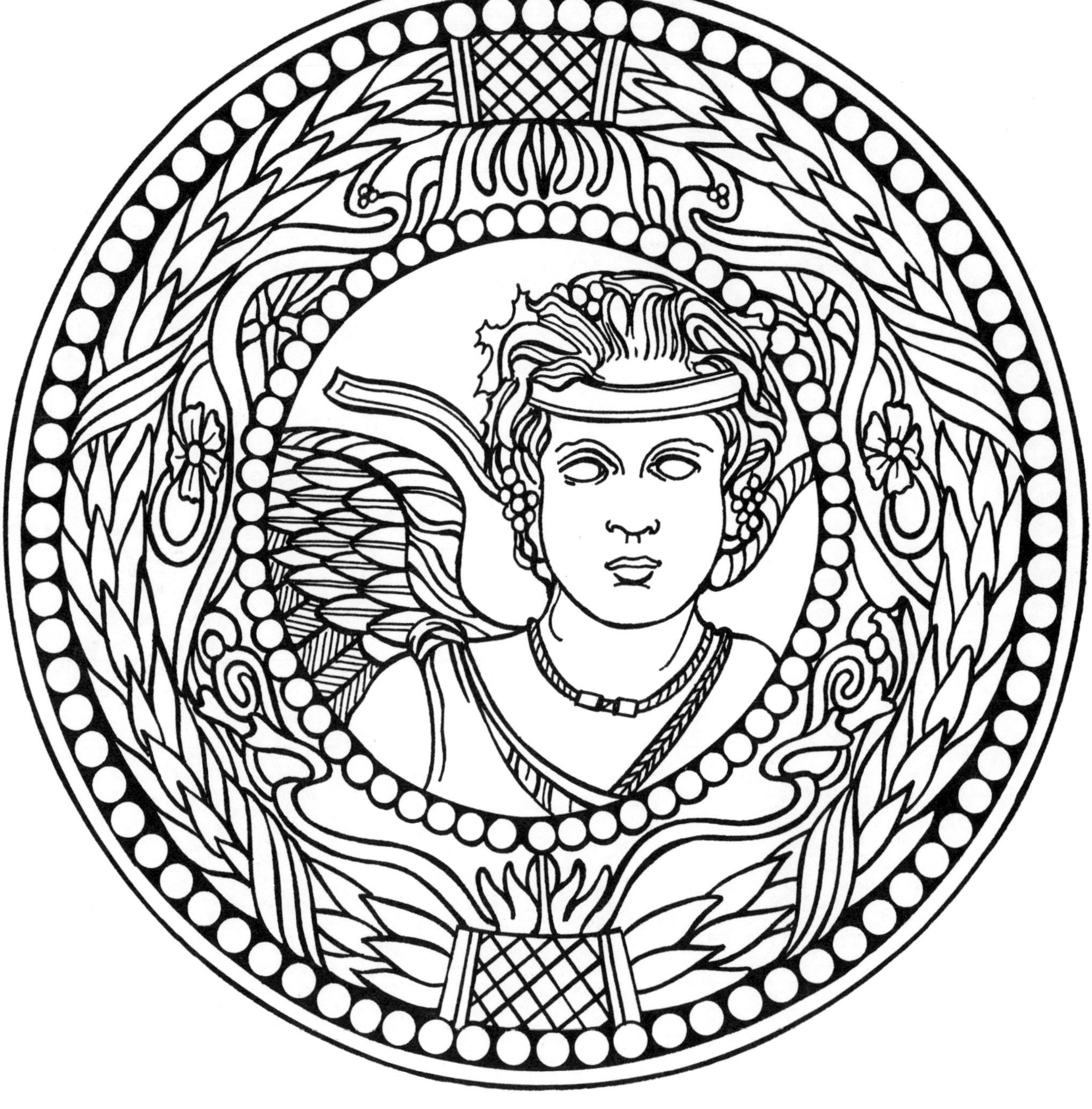

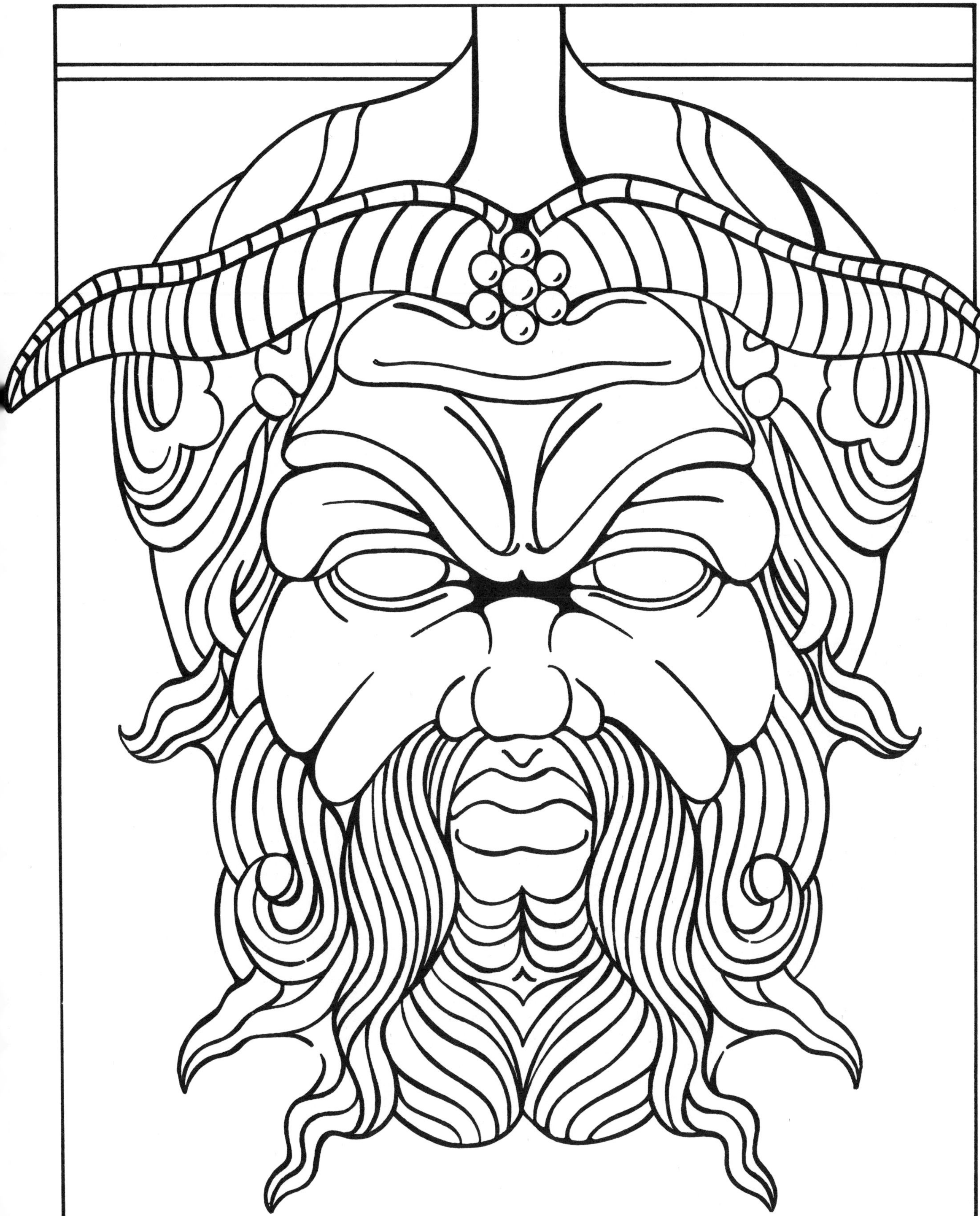

Designed by Barbara Holdridge
Composed in Times Roman by Brown Composition, Inc.,
Baltimore, Maryland
Printed on 75-pound Williamsburg Offset paper and
bound by Hagerstown Bookbinding and Printing
Company, Inc., Hagerstown, Maryland
Cover color-separated by GraphTec, Baltimore, Maryland
and printed by Hagerstown Bookbinding and Printing
Company, Inc., Hagerstown, Maryland